Context & Content

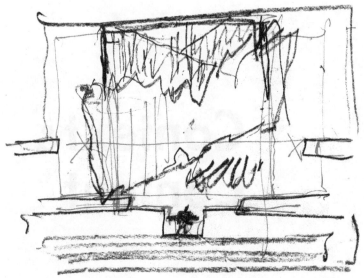

Conceptual design: Le Grand Orgue Pierre-Béique

Context & Content

The Memoir of a Fortunate Architect

A.J. Diamond

DUNDURN
PRESS

Publisher and acquiring editor: Scott Fraser | Editor: Laurie Miller
Interior designer: Laura Boyle
Cover designer: A.J. Diamond
Cover image: Tom Arban Photography; image editing by Elizabeth Gyde
Interior images: Courtesy of the author, except courtesy of Stella Gentin: *Simma Gittle Werner (née Liebel)*; *Rabbi Werner (seated, right), at Zionist Congress, Basle, 1898*; *Rabbi Werner's funeral, London, 1912*

Library and Archives Canada Cataloguing in Publication

Title: Context & content : the memoir of a fortunate architect / A.J. Diamond.
Other titles: Context and content
Names: Diamond, A. J. (Abel Joseph), 1932- author.
Identifiers: Canadiana (print) 20210389117 | Canadiana (ebook) 20210389206 | ISBN 9781459749764 (softcover) | ISBN 9781459749771 (PDF) | ISBN 9781459749788 (EPUB)
Subjects: LCSH: Diamond, A. J. (Abel Joseph), 1932- | LCSH: Architects—Canada—Biography. | LCGFT: Autobiographies.
Classification: LCC NA749.D52 A2 2022 | DDC 720.92—dc23

We acknowledge the support of the Canada Council for the Arts and the Ontario Arts Council for our publishing program. We also acknowledge the financial support of the Government of Ontario, through the Ontario Book Publishing Tax Credit and Ontario Creates, and the Government of Canada.

Care has been taken to trace the ownership of copyright material used in this book. The author and the publisher welcome any information enabling them to rectify any references or credits in subsequent editions.

The publisher is not responsible for websites or their content unless they are owned by the publisher.

Printed and bound in Canada.

Dundurn Press
1382 Queen Street East
Toronto, Ontario, Canada M4L 1C9
dundurn.com, @dundurnpress 🐦 f 📷

To Gillian, Andrew, and Suki

If opportunity doesn't knock, build a door.
— MILTON BERLE

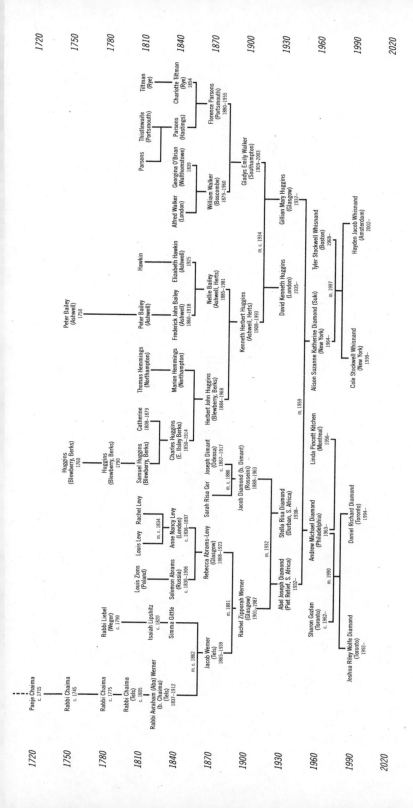

Prologue

WHEN I WAS NINE YEARS OLD I FOUND A WOODEN PALETTE in our banana plantation. It was made of planks nailed to a wattle pole frame, about five feet by seven. Peter, the family gardener, helped me carry it the kilometre to our house.

Using ropes, Peter helped me hoist the platform up into a large pine tree. I could see that the horizontal branches were perfect: first, to make brackets for supporting my house, and, second, to make the stairs I would need to climb up to it. The rest I did alone. I fixed short posts along the perimeter, then wove sticks, basket-like, around three sides of it. When I lay down in my tree house — the first house of my own making — I was invisible to anyone on the ground or in the main house.

The satisfaction I felt at this accomplishment has stayed with me. I can still feel the pleasant burning sensation in my palms — physical labour, the first I can remember — and the exaltation of first imagining and then creating this secure and secret place. The pallet had become something wonderful because of my hands, my imagination, and my work. It was a quantum leap from my previous efforts: blankets arranged over upturned chairs, corrugated cardboard nailed to banana trees.

It was a breakthrough, but it didn't last. My father discovered my house, thought it dangerous, and had Peter throw it to the ground. The shock of that act of destruction — and my rage — has also stayed with me. I eventually persuaded my parents to let me rebuild the tree house, but it was never the same.

I spend long hours now travelling by jet. These are hours in which the eye turns inward, hours in which I sometimes design imaginary houses for myself in places I have recently seen, or in conjured landscapes, evolutions of that first imagined tree house. I fill the blank pages at the end of books I am reading with these designs. It is a way, I suppose, of achieving order.

It is hard to describe the satisfaction of achieving a sense of order at any scale. That satisfaction is balm to the soul. The analogy that best describes this is when a magnet is passed below a sheet of paper on which iron filings are randomly scattered: the filings immediately conform to a magnetic order. That's what happens when I get a drawing, or a painting, or, most of all, the design of a building, just right. It is coherence of a transcendental nature. My filings lined up in cosmic conformity.

Throughout my career, I have attempted to make a positive impact: designing buildings that are environmentally responsible and appropriate to their context; favouring urban configurations that promote safety, enhance urban cohesion, and respect the human scale; promoting cities that effectively address land use, transportation, and good governance. The satisfaction I have derived from doing so has been profound.

I have often observed that most people want to be engaged in something greater than themselves — even to the extent of giving their lives to a noble cause. Architects are no exception. We have both the expertise and the opportunity to address the man-made world and its social content to great effect. Opportunities abound. Whether social, physical, or moral, there is hardly a project in which these factors are not present. Such engagement not only benefits others, but provides infinite personal fulfillment in contributing to positive change. We can, as the Old Testament decrees, *tikkun olam*: "make a better world."

One

The Mariinsky II Theatre, Saint Petersburg, Russia

IN DECEMBER 2007, A DINNER WAS ARRANGED FOR VALERY Gergiev, the Russian conductor who was conducting a Stravinsky program with the Mariinsky Orchestra in Toronto's Roy Thomson Hall. Gergiev had been given a tour of the Four Seasons Centre for the Performing Arts by the conductor Richard Bradshaw, had admired its acoustics and architecture (and modest budget), and expressed interest in meeting the architect. Bob Ramsay was giving the dinner for Gergiev, and I was invited.

I was seated next to Valery, and we discussed opera houses and concert halls. We had similar views. It was an engaging conversation but by 1:30 a.m. I was tired and excused myself, saying I had an early morning. Gergiev said he had to work later that day, as well.

"What are you doing?" I asked.

"Conducting *War and Peace* at the Met this evening," he said.

Six months later, Valery invited me to New York to continue our conversation. He showed me some of the design options for a second opera house in Saint Petersburg. The original Mariinsky Theatre was built in 1860 and is one of the legendary opera houses in the world. The plan was to build a second opera house — the Mariinsky II. It would be the most important design project built in Russia in the last seventy years. It was important for several reasons. There hadn't been much interesting new architecture in Russia, and it was important as a symbol. Putin was one year into his prime ministership and the country was struggling economically, awkwardly poised between capitalism and communism. Russia had very little cultural imprint outside its own borders. The shining exception was Gergiev, who was conductor of both the Mariinsky Theatre Orchestra and the London Symphony Orchestra, and a regular guest conductor at the Met. In the classical world, he had the status of a rock star.

He was also a friend of Vladimir Putin; they'd met when Putin was deputy mayor of Saint Petersburg. The intention was to make the city one of the world's great cultural centres, which would include the original Mariinsky Theatre, a small concert hall called the Mariinsky III, a rehabilitation of the surrounding area, and a new centrepiece — the Mariinsky II. A great deal was invested in the project. It already had a troubled, complex history worthy of Kafka, and I would soon find myself part of the story.

It had begun in 2001, when a tender for the project was won by American developers who retained Californian architect Eric Owen Moss. His scheme used water and ice as a theme, reflecting Saint Petersburg's canals and impressive winter. It was a radical design that met with disapproval from local politicians and architects.

It was then decided to hold an international competition, with eleven architects invited to submit proposals, among them Moss. In 2003, it was announced that French architect Dominque Perrault had won the competition. Perrault's design had a gold glass canopy that he described as "a sort of veil." It, too, was radical, but also impractical. He suggested using robots to clean all that glass. In private Putin suggested the design looked like a giant condom.

Clearly, the building was intended to echo the so-called Bilbao effect, a somewhat simplistic notion that a single dramatic building could transform a city. Even Frank Gehry had repudiated that idea. The Russians wanted something bold, but they also wanted something that would be sensitive to Saint Petersburg's historical context.

It was a complicated time for both architecture and Russia. The oligarchs appeared to be running wild with the idea of capitalism, there was war in Chechnya, and there was domestic terrorism. A 2004 poll asked, "What social institution do you most trust?" Results showed 28 percent trusted no one; 50 percent trusted Putin, though only 1 percent trusted political parties; 14 percent trusted the Russian Orthodox Church; 9 the army; 9 the government; 5 the police; and 3 the trade unions. A particularly Russian poll: its numbers totalled 119 percent.

When Valery showed me Perrault's design, I thought it was more concerned with spectacle than the demands of an opera house: those of acoustics, the performing space, and the audience experience. Perrault himself described it as "very fashionable." It was also considered unbuildable. I thought it would result in high operating costs and be a cultural embarrassment, viewed as kitsch within a decade.

I wasn't alone in my assessment. Russia's byzantine regulatory system found more than four hundred infractions in the design. "The criticism is of a serious nature," said a spokesman for the Northwestern Directorate for the Construction, Reconstruction, and Restoration of Saint Petersburg. "It concerns the building's stability, its safety, and the absence of coordination between different parts of the projects done by various subcontractors."

Perrault was fired in January 2007, dismissed by the Federal Agency for Culture and Cinematography (one of many departments that have a say in cultural buildings) as a contractor who did not meet his obligations. Perrault responded that this was an illustration of how difficult it was to work in Russia and of the challenges of its legendary bureaucracy.

I would soon get to experience it first-hand. I met with Valery in New York where he was staying at the Phillips Club, near the Met. Wherever he was it seemed as if he was holding court. Musicians, recording artists, donors, and others in some way related to musical performances came and went as we talked. While he held court, I noticed he had his tea (with no milk) in a glass, and used honey instead of sugar. It was exactly as my grandfather took his tea, though my grandfather had thin slices of apple in the tea, as well. While Valery did not divulge the parlous state of his own efforts to build a new opera house in Saint Petersburg, he did intimate that he was interested in holding another competition. He invited me to Saint Petersburg to view the site. On June 10, 2007, I flew to Russia.

. . .

Saint Petersburg astonished me. The terrible depredations of the Second World War were nowhere visible; the city had been beautifully restored to its former neoclassical glory. The consistency of scale and materials is unmatched by any city I know, including Venice, Jerusalem, Bath, and Paris. Most streets are lined with buildings that vary between four and six storeys, most in stucco, some in stone, consistently coloured a pale yellow or other warm pastel shade, with white columns and window trim. This cohesion is occasionally dramatically contrasted by exceptional free-standing structures, such as the onion-domed, exuberantly coloured (and named) Cathedral of the Spilled Blood, and the monumental Kazan and St. Isaac's cathedrals. There are also a series of beautiful, smaller, stucco churches, such as St. Nicholas — blue and white with bright gilded spires.

During the design and construction of the Mariinsky II, I would make nineteen trips to Saint Petersburg. Occasionally, I would visit the elegant blue and gold St. Nicholas church on the Kryukov Canal, a short distance from our site. Sometimes I went to the monumental St. Isaac's cathedral. I went to hear the music of the Orthodox Church, especially the heart-stirring *basso profundo* at which the Russians excel. I am an atheist, but the power of that music is something that resonates in me. It's as if my physical being is transformed into a spiritual one.

Clearly, the design problem for any architect working in Saint Petersburg is to find a contemporary expression of the principles upon which the city was built. If the new opera house was to be part of the city aggregate, it would need to maintain its continuity and scale. If it was to be a free-standing structure, as the churches and cathedrals are, it could then contrast with its context.

That night I attended a performance of Glinka's opera *A Life for the Tsar* at the Mariinsky Theatre, and I wondered what my grandfather, Joseph Dimant, would have thought about this. He was killed in Russian Lithuania in the First World War during the chaotic retreat of the Russian army when militia were laying waste to the country, raping at will and killing Jews. Now seated in the Czar's box, I confess to experiencing a profound sense of triumph.

I had never heard an orchestra play with such cohesion nor seen a conductor in such control, and this was accomplished without any extravagant gestures. It was nearing the summer solstice, and when I came out of the theatre, it was still light. It was one of Saint Petersburg's famous white nights, when, during the summer, the sun hardly sets.

The site for the new Mariinsky was vast. In Europe and North America, scene construction, costume storage, and other back-of-house functions are accommodated in low-rent industrial buildings somewhere on a city's perimeter; but in Saint Petersburg they would all be located within the opera-house complex itself. With the auditorium, five stages, opera and ballet rehearsal rooms, and public areas, it added up to some ninety thousand square metres. It would essentially occupy an entire city block, bounded by the Kryukov Canal, on which the old Mariinsky is located, by Decembrist Street, and by apartment buildings on the other two perimeters.

The next morning I had breakfast with Valery in his penthouse apartment overlooking the Neva River and we talked about the new Mariinsky. He asked me to design it.

"Draw me a picture," he said.
"I don't work like that," I replied.
"I need pictures to show Putin."

. . .

I returned to Toronto, and with my team of Matthew Lella, Michael Treacy, Gary McCluskie, and Michael Lukasik, developed a scheme in five weeks. This efficiency was based on our experience in designing and building the Four Seasons Centre for the Performing Arts, the Canadian Opera Company's home in Toronto, and my lifelong interest in acoustics and concert halls. Concert halls and their acoustics was the subject of the thesis for my Bachelor of Architecture degree. I had been supremely lucky — the visiting professor at the School of Architecture in the University of Cape Town at the time was Philip Hope Bagenal, the English acoustician. He became my thesis supervisor and mentor. Hope's principle was to allow the physics of sound to determine an auditorium's shape, and the materials, texture, and configuration of its every surface.

When Valery saw the drawings, he said, "Be bolder." It was the classic dilemma of wanting something bold, but also wanting something that would fit into the existing streetscape. The boldness of the first design by Eric Owen Moss had prompted Saint Petersburg's chief architect, Oleg Kharchenko, to say it was a repudiation of Russian history. "You who have lived in this city for so long, your ancestors who created this city, you did it all the wrong way. Your design is empty nonsense." Perrault met with similar criticism for his version.

My aim was to design an uncompromisingly contemporary building, but one also in harmony with Saint Petersburg's historic past. Two approaches were considered. The first would be a free-standing structure, like the extravagant cathedrals and churches that stand in dynamic contrast to the background of consistent, continuous streetscapes characteristic of the city. However, the new Mariinsky had to accommodate both performance and production functions. This would occupy the entire block of land designated for the new opera house. Consequently, a free-standing structure was out of the question.

The alternative was to design a building that would be both a harmonious aggregate to the city's historic urbanity and be distinguished from it. As is often the case, the design has to resolve seemingly irreconcilably opposing factors.

The result was to continue the scale of the surrounding streets; with stone facades in a pale rose colour; a metal roof to provide a canopy for the rooftop amphitheatre; vertical fenestration in syncopated rather than regular rhythm; and a large glass bay over the principal entrance, instead of a classical portico. Most significant were the views of the interior through the vertical fenestration: what is visible is a four-storey, backlit, onyx, curvilinear auditorium-enclosing wall. This gives a subtle yet powerful indicator of the distinction that an opera house justifies. Both harmony with the surroundings and distinction for the building would be achieved.

· · ·

By now we had, in effect, the commission to design the new Mariinsky, but we'd received it from a user, Valery Gergiev, not from the Ministry of Culture, which was formally the client. And, unbeknownst to us, another version was already being constructed. A theatrical supply company — TDM — held the contract to supply the Mariinsky with all its stage and auditorium equipment, and they had hired German acoustician Jürgen Reinhold of Müller-BBM for the project. Jürgen asked who the architect was, and was told, "We don't have one," so Müller-BBM hired an Italian firm — Alvisi Kirimoto + Partners — who modified Perrault's scheme.

Our first video conference with the ViPS Group (the Russian engineering and architecture firm with which we were obliged to collaborate, and who were acting as the architect of record, even though it was mostly an engineering firm occupied with oil wells, mining, and other industrial structures), was a somewhat surreal experience: We tried to present our drawings but were rebuffed by ViPS. "There is no point in showing us these drawings," they said, "because we have an auditorium design and we are building it."

We responded that we were now the architects, and there was a new design. After four hours of futility, it became clear that ViPS had no interest in wading back into the bureaucracy to get new contracts, new approvals, and new signatures from the party holdovers who populated the government offices. They were going to continue to work, following the Italian firm's version of the Perrault design. The Perrault design had been repudiated in the strongest terms, but the bureaucracy reigns supreme. They had official approval for the Kirimoto design. So their scheme would proceed uninterrupted.

As we did not have a contract or an official client, we couldn't even get the fire or building codes. For several months we had largely fruitless talks with various Russians. During one video conference with ViPS people, Christopher Pomorski, the deputy director of ViPS, solemnly announced, "Jack Diamond is ambitious man. Every architect is ambitious. Some people in Saint Petersburg, they are also ambitious." A particularly Russian message: tread carefully.

We were rescued, more or less, by Putin. In 2009, he declared that yet another competition for the Mariinsky would be held. We were put in the odd position of entering a design for a project we thought we already had. We were among the five finalists, along with a German firm and three Russian firms. In July, an open, public presentation of the competition entries was held in the spacious lobby of the city architect's building. It was filled to capacity. My sense was that we were not facing a friendly audience. Nonetheless, we were acclaimed the winners. We were no longer naive enough to think this was the end of our problems.

. . .

It turned out the competition was only for the exterior envelope of the building. The mechanics and lobby were still being worked on by ViPS. It was absurd to marry our envelope to someone else's interior, but this was the compromise that had been arrived at, without our input. Meanwhile, the rejected Perrault version was still being constructed.

However, working in our favour, Saint Petersburg is built on a swamp, and bedrock is thirty-six metres below grade. Sinking the piles for Perrault's design was a time-consuming challenge. There was also a shortage of construction and design expertise for opera houses in Russia, a fact of which they were not unaware.

The hybrid design formed by ViPs, the equipment supply company, the German acousticians, and Perrault, had been approved by the Expertisers, the governing body in Moscow that grants building permits. I explained to the Expertisers that we had just won the design competition to build a new opera house. "That may be so," I was told, "but you have not had Expertiser approval. You should now submit your drawings for approval." Construction of the foundation had risen to twelve metres below grade at this point. I figured we could still adapt our design to a foundation at eight metres below grade. We didn't achieve Expertiser approval until the workers were at four metres below the surface. The successful adaptation of our design to the foundation of a completely different scheme was one of the greatest, and entirely unseen, design feats we accomplished in Saint Petersburg.

The key to a concert hall, besides the back-of-house technology, is the auditorium, its acoustics, and its sightlines. It was the acoustics that Valery had so admired in the Four Seasons opera house. Now that aspect was being jeopardized by the fact that ViPS had taken control of it. Optimistically, we continued to work on our own design for the lobby and auditorium. So there were two parallel versions being designed. We tried to get a meeting with the minister of culture to plead our case, but it was cancelled at the last minute, an ominous sign. On November 17, 2009, ViPS called me and said that their own version was now definitively the official one.

I immediately called Valery, who was about to go onstage. "I think Mr. Putin has to put his foot down," I said. "Someone is trying to sabotage us."

I called ViPS back. We had hired a Russian-trained architect in Toronto, Marina Moukhortova, who translated. The conversation resembled a Cold War film where nuclear missiles have been fired.

"They say they have reached the point of no return," Marina said. More rapid Russian. "There is a state-issued contract. It has never happened in Russian reality to walk away from a state project." She also said the ministry thought our scheme was too expensive and would have inferior acoustics, which was ridiculous.

In December 2009, I wrote a letter to the minister of culture, Aleksandr Alekseyevich Avdeyev, telling him that our design would have better acoustics and sightlines (some of the ViPS seats had no view of the stage whatsoever), and if they went with an inferior design, we would withdraw from the project. The ministry held firm to the ViPS design. I asked for a mediator and Valery called on Herman Gref, the CEO of Sberbank, Russia's largest bank, and chairman of the Mariinsky board. Gref appointed his VP, Andrey Stroev, to mediate.

In January 2010, we went to Moscow for a showdown in the boardroom of the Sberbank headquarters. On one side, ViPS and the Northwestern Directorate for the Construction, Reconstruction, and Restoration of Saint Petersburg. On the other side, Gary McCluskie and I, flanked by Jürgen Reinhold, the German acoustician; Josh Dachs, of Fisher Dachs, the theatre consultants from New York; and our Toronto engineers. As a member of our firm would note, "ViPS are clearly lost in their own design with no idea how to achieve the basic balance of requirement for sightlines, balcony apertures, and room form, but they resist taking on our design solution. It is partly pride and control that holds them back from adopting our solution, but more fundamental is a lack of imagination. They don't really understand the complexity of the room design." A fair representation of our view of ViPS's work.

The Russian resistance to outside influence goes back more than a century. In his 1864 novel *Notes from Underground*, published four years after the first Mariinsky was built, Dostoevsky wrote about the influence of the West on Russian culture. "Why, everything, unquestionably almost everything we have — of development, science, art, civic-mindedness, humanity, everything, everything comes from there — from that same land of holy wonders!"

The meeting covered a lot of ground: The minister of culture asked me if we could have a classical architecture facade. I explained that authentic architecture made no distinction between interior and exterior — all cohesion would be lost by such a division. Gref also attended our presentation, and I could sense his support. We were asked to leave the room and to wait outside. In the end, we were re-awarded the design. On February 1, the ministry issued the signed Design Task documents and our design officially proceeded.

$$\cdot \quad \cdot \quad \cdot$$

In June 2010, we were back in Saint Petersburg for an acrimonious meeting with our Russian colleagues, and with the Directorate, which was late in making our fee payments. The federal government has two accounts with the Directorate, one for construction, one for fee payment. The former is funded, the latter is not. We were also surprised to learn that our joint-venture company had in fact been "lending" money to the Directorate, our state client, to pay the Expertisers, who had charged ahead with the Perrault design.

The Russians look like us, but they are not like us. Their culture, and their building culture, are vastly different from ours. There is an irony in the fact that the cumbersome system designed to prevent corruption provides ample opportunity to do just that. We met the deputy minister of culture, a bear of a man who smoked cigarette after cigarette but who was astonishingly perceptive and turned out to be a valuable ally in the ongoing trench war. Russian meetings, like Russian novels, tend to be long — 10:00 a.m. to 8:00 p.m. without a lunch break.

The White Nights Festival meant Saint Petersburg was crowded — performances and festivities go on almost all night. It was difficult getting around the city, a difficulty made worse when traffic is blocked to let some VIP sail through. We met with Valery, then watched him conduct a performance of a Prokofiev opera — appropriately for us, *The Gambler*. It started late and at intermission we visited Valery again, amid the hordes vying for his attention. His driver/bodyguard Michael stood outside Valery's office/dressing room, and only the privileged were allowed in. During one intermission Valery was watching World Cup soccer on TV, but it was the only chance we got to discuss urgent design issues with him.

· · ·

We visited the site in early April 2011, and again near the end of May. There was no longer snow on the ground, but the site was chaotic — poor material management, low standard of concrete strength, and very little progress. Concrete subcontractors in Russia are paid by the volume of concrete poured, so they concentrate on low-strength heavy walls and slabs and neglect the more delicate and complex structural forms. The point man at the Directorate had no knowledge of construction and had never been responsible for a large project of any kind, and the contractor visited the site once a week at most. The site was a mess, with inaccurate concrete pours — columns in some instances did not line up floor over floor! One thing the contractor was skilled at was pointing the blame elsewhere. At the rate they were going, the building wouldn't be ready by the scheduled 2012 date. We had a meeting the next day and concluded that the job was out of control.

The DSAI (Diamond Schmitt Architects Inc.) design team usually stayed at the Astoria Hotel. While not as grand as the Grand, it was the hotel Tolstoy stayed in on the rare occasions he visited the city. Right next to St. Issac's Cathedral, an easy walk to the Mariinsky. On this walk one passes the house in which Nabokov's family lived, and the Yusupov Palace, in which Rasputin was assassinated before being dumped into the canal right outside the front door.

The elevators in the Astoria were lined with small brass plates with the names of notables who have stayed in the hotel. I was surprised to see that mine was included. I took it as a good omen, even though it was my colleagues who had arranged this.

Our visits to Saint Petersburg consisted of long meetings, bad traffic, and dealing with the bureaucracy. There were meetings with Valery, but he was often en route from one conducting assignment to another, and wasn't always easy to nail down.

My efforts to change the contractor and the Directorate's project manager finally bore fruit in March 2012. Metrostroy, a large construction company, replaced the existing construction company, GKS. They had a solid reputation, but their experience was in building subways and highways and other heavy civil engineering projects. The new project manager was Marat Oganesyan. With the last project manager, we had to push him to get on with construction. Now we had the opposite problem; Oganesyan pushed so hard that I worried that the quality of construction might suffer. Architects have relatively little power in Russia, and we had few means of exercising quality control. Our salvation would be having experienced, sophisticated, foreign subcontractors for all the finishing work. It would compensate for the crudeness of the underlying concrete structure. But given the budget constraints, occasioned by previous profligate waste (and who knows where the money went), I knew we would have a battle awarding contracts to foreign suppliers, which would be more expensive.

Nevertheless, we managed to make a number of decisions regarding materials, balcony fronts, and seating, which would hopefully result in the realization of our design. The herculean efforts of Michael Treacy and Mike Lukasik on the detailing, preparation, and recording of all requirements made it possible. Michael visited the manufacturer of the auditorium seating in Milan, and selected the actual marble, granite, and onyx at an Italian quarry. Making direct contact with the suppliers was an insurance policy against the supply of inferior products. I insisted that nothing should be installed without either my signature on the product, or that of a member of our core team. Mike Lukasik, who camped in ViPS office for weeks at a time, did a superb job of detailing every aspect of the project.

. . .

Due to Oganesyan's pushing, it was now possible to project an opening date of June 2013. But new, unforeseen hurdles continued to arise. The minister of culture wished to appoint an architect for the interiors! What could this possibly mean? The subcontracts for furniture, seating, floor, and wall finishes had already been let out. We had learned that Ms. Medvedev, wife of Dmitry Medvedev, the Russian prime minister, was interested in interior design, but liked historical styles, not contemporary ones. Could she be behind this? It would have had to come from high up to effect change this late in the game.

I flew to Saint Petersburg in May 2012 and was told that dinner with Marat Oganesyan, the project manager, had been cancelled; not a good sign. I called Valery, who was in London conducting a mammoth open-air concert in Trafalgar Square, who confirmed a meeting for the following Wednesday.

Before the meeting I toured the site, which showed great progress. The roof was capped and the focus was on particular rooms, to ready them for a face-saving "soft opening" on June 21, the given completion date, as the opening of the whole project was months off. The choir rehearsal room would be where the soft-opening concert would take place, with a second concert for Russian notables. We couldn't open in time, but we could at least use some part of the building. In this way, the projected 2012 opening date was met.

I met with Marat, who told me that the minister of culture had recently opened a classically styled concert hall in a provincial town and was impressed by the interiors. They were designed by a Russian artist named Yuri Kuper, who had been popular in the 1970s. The minister wanted him involved. Marat was as reluctant as we were to make any changes, but said if the instruction came from on high, he would have to follow it. We then met with Valery, who was about to conduct a concert. When I asked him how seriously we should take this request, he replied, "Very seriously."

I was somewhat relieved to find that this latest request only extended to the design of the curtain, though we had already retained a graphic artist and textile designer to develop a contemporary design. The minister, Aleksandr Alekseyevich Avdeyev, appeared at 7:15, with Yuri Kuper in tow. The concert in the Mariinsky III was scheduled for 7:00 p.m. but would start late, as concerts often do in Russia. The minister, whom I had written to but hadn't seen since the decisive meeting in Moscow, was charming, and now said admiring things about the design. At 7:30 Valery said he should get dressed for the concert or the audience would start rhythmic clapping, which is how they demonstrate impatience. A documentary about Gergiev is entitled *You Cannot Start Without Me.* Valery suggested we continue our discussion during the intermission.

The Austrian ambassador to Russia then arrived with her entourage and asked Valery if he would include Austrian works in the 2013 summer festival, which was to be the year of Austria in Russia. Not the first time Austria has been in Russia, though not always for cultural events.

We weren't able to resolve anything at the concert, so scheduled a meeting for 10:00 a.m. the next day, at which the minister of culture now declared our design boring, merely a computer design. He felt the predominant feature of Saint Petersburg was water and that should be the theme of the curtain. And it was a tradition, he said, that Russians designed the curtains for Russian theatres.

It was non-Russians that Peter the Great had called in to design his city, though I didn't say that. Instead, I said we should look forward rather than try to replicate the successes of the past. The minister said that looking forward was a Bolshevik stance. I could have replied that it was also a Bolshevik characteristic to determine what is acceptable art, but didn't. Instead, I said that I was of Russian descent (my grandparents on both maternal and paternal sides were Lithuanian citizens of Russia), and that the minister, as a former diplomat (to France), would recognize our conversation as a "frank exchange of views." In the end, a particularly Russian solution — appointing a committee made up of the minister, Valery, two others, and myself to resolve the problem. Unsurprisingly, Kuper's curtain design of a large feather over water was selected.

Putin's support of Valery and the Mariinsky in Saint Petersburg (Putin's native city) was essential to the project. To demonstrate progress and in appreciation of Putin's support, Valery held a dinner for him, appropriately, in the Czar's dining room in the original opera house. There were about a dozen notables around the dinner table, among them Herman Gref of Sperbank. The airspace around Saint Petersburg was closed for an hour before Putin arrived and for an hour after he left. Cars were prohibited from the streets around the Mariinsky, and there was a security guard at every door in the building.

Valery invited some of us to say something. Putin had an interpreter for those who spoke English. I assumed he did not speak English. I said it was an honour to contribute to Russia's great cultural tradition (a genuine one for me), especially in the performing arts. Putin generously thanked me for my contribution.

The next time I met Putin was at the gala opening performance of Mariinsky II, a grand affair with selections from the Mariinsky's vast repertoire, chosen to demonstrate the extraordinary technology of the new house. The performance was perfection; soloists, chorus, orchestra, and ballet of quite another order. Putin said to me in perfect English, "You know,

Italian architects designed Saint Petersburg and the Kremlin; that is a state building like this new opera house. They did a good job, as you have done here. We did not let them leave the country."

Two

Beginnings and Endings

I WAS BORN IN MY GRANDFATHER'S LIBRARY IN PIET Retief, in South Africa's Eastern Transvaal. It was, and probably still is, a dusty provincial town. The library had been made by enclosing a porch across the end of the house with windows. Bookshelves lined the solid end wall of the house. It was strewn with two or three zebra hides. There were two reimpi (made by a mesh of thin hide strips) chairs, and a divan that was covered by a kaross — a throw made of the skins of smaller antelope sewn together.

My parents lived in Cedarville, in East Griqualand, a village that was even smaller than Piet Retief. One of my earliest memories is going with my father by car to the station to collect the newspapers that were thrown onto the platform by the passing express train — Cedarville didn't warrant a stop by every train. The raised station platform sloped toward the rail line, and my father drove the car onto it, at right angles to the train track. He left me in the car and chatted with the station master while waiting for the express and its bundle of newspapers. He must have left the car in gear, because when I pushed the starter button out of curiosity, the car lurched forward. I can remember the look of panicked terror on my father's face as he ran to pull on the hand brake just in time. The express roared by a few feet away, its terrifying bulk followed by silence and relief.

The circuit court periodically met in Cedarville, with its accompaniment of magistrates, judges, court clerks, lawyers, and policemen. The policemen were mounted, and wore imposing gear — spiked khaki pith helmets, leather leggings, chrome spurs, and chains to secure the spurs to their highly polished boots. After court was adjourned each day, the court officials and policemen would sit on our long verandah for a "sundowner." The horses were tethered to posts in front of the hotel. My Basuto nanny used the police to frighten me into obedience, saying that if I misbehaved they would punish me. With my nanny's dire warnings in my imagination, the sight of this assembled cavalry terrified me. One day I fled and hid in the back of a car in the garage and was found only hours later.

To overcome this fear, my father took me to the police post where the sergeant put me on his knee and gave me a bar of chocolate. I wasn't so easily fooled — it wasn't hard to figure out where the chocolate came from.

. . .

Avraham (Aba) Werner, my great-grandfather, after whom I am named, was rabbi of Machzike Hadath Synagogue on Brick Lane in London's East End from 1891 until 1912. Anglo-Jewry underwent a profound change both in structure and character as a result of the large immigration from Eastern Europe at the turn of the century. Thousands of orthodox Russian and Polish Jews fleeing Czarist pogroms arrived in London. The synagogue was opposite a Nicholas Hawksmoor mannerist church. Originally the synagogue was a church built by Huguenot immigrants in the early eighteenth century, then was converted to a Methodist chapel, then to a synagogue after the Huguenots prospered and moved out of the East End. It is now a madrassa.

My great-grandfather, who had changed his name from Chaima to Werner so that Russian agents would not be able to track his illegal emigration, is buried in Edmonton, U.K. His wife, Simma Gittle, who died in 1906, is buried next to him. Matching tombstones mark their graves. The gravesite of my paternal grandfather, Joseph Dimant, is unknown, but is probably in Rosseini, Lithuania. He was murdered by Russian soldiers in 1917, a militia that ravaged the Baltic states. The grave of his wife, Sarah Risa, is also unknown, but presumably is in Lithuania, as well. Jacob Werner, my maternal grandfather, son of rabbi Aba Werner, emigrated to South Africa in the early 1890s. He married Rachel Levy, a Glaswegian. Both are buried in Piet Retief. My mother was born in Glasgow in 1901 on a family return visit from South Africa. Jacob and Rachel Zipporah Diamond, my parents, are buried in Durban, South Africa. My maternal forebears were spared the Holocaust, unlike my father's family, most of whom remained in Europe.

• • •

My father, Jacob Dimant, began his immigrant odyssey in Rosseini, Kovno Giberna, (County Kovno, now Kaunas) Lithuania. He left at sixteen to avoid being drafted into the Czar's army, which then occupied Lithuania, and emigrated to South Africa. This must have been the winter of 1901 or 1902. His parents, and those of a few of his companions, had bribed the border guards to let their boys cross the frontier; it was illegal to leave the country without permission. Unfortunately, the guard had been changed when they arrived at the border, so they spent a freezing day and night in a forest until the guard was changed back the next day. The boys then took a train to Hamburg, and bought steerage passage to Cape Town. The blanket and cookies Jacob's mother, Sarah Risa, had given him for the journey were promptly stolen on board.

My paternal grandfather's brother had previously emigrated to South Africa and had anglicized his surname from Dimant to Diamond. For family consistency, my father did the same upon arriving in Cape Town. He arrived with no English and few skills, although his immigration papers state his profession as photographer. The languages he spoke — Russian, Polish, Lithuanian, Yiddish, and German — were of little help, although the Yiddish and German made learning Afrikaans easy.

He managed to get a job with a jeweller selling a popular gold brooch that featured a miniature pick, panning tray, and gold nugget. He sold them to passengers on the Union and Castle liners that brought tourists to the Cape. He also sold tubes of ostrich feathers. After three months, he took half his salary in kind and half in cash, to begin trading on his own. He bought a bicycle, and in six months was entirely on his own.

Ostrich feathers were a great and fashionable luxury, and like gold, mostly came from South Africa. The ostrich farmers of the Karoo, the semi-desert area that lies to the east of the fertile southwest Cape, supplied the fashion houses of the world's capitals with the finest feathers. The feather market was in Cape Town. My father went from selling feathers to tourists to buying the product directly in the feather exchange, to trading feathers as a commodity, and finally to breeding ostriches and producing the feathers himself on properties he bought in the Karoo. His feel for feathers was literal — he once gave evidence as an expert witness in an ostrich-rustling trial, where he was blindfolded and still able to distinguish between feathers from different districts in the Karoo. His skills and entrepreneurship earned him a partnership, at the age of twenty-three, in one of the two major ostrich-feather producers in Oudtshoorn, the principal ostrich farming district of the Karoo. Joseph, Hotz and Diamond were represented in Paris, London, New York, and Montevideo.

He had a smart trap drawn by a pair of matched dapple-grey horses. On buying trips, farmers would put him up overnight, as there were no other places to stay in those remote rural areas. The farmers welcomed his visits; being Jewish he was revered, as Afrikaner farmers of that generation were stalwart members of the Dutch Reformed Church, and the Old Testament was central to their faith. The Jews were the Chosen People (*"For you are a people holy to the LORD your God; the LORD your God has chosen you to be a people for his own possession, out of all the peoples that are on the face of the earth"*).

He would spend three or four hours a day in the saddle while farming ostrich and, later, sheep, and his love of that life never left him.

Before the First World War, ostrich feathers were a more lucrative commodity than gold, and my father saw little need to diversify. He was able to bring his parents to South Africa for a tour, although they didn't take to Africa and returned to Lithuania. My father never told me that his father was killed in a pogrom in 1917. I learned that from my cousin Esther. Of my father's family contemporaries, she and her sister were the only survivors of Belsen concentration camp. Esther's husband was taken away by the S.S. at 2:00 a.m. and never seen again. Her two children, a boy of eleven and a nine-year-old daughter, whose names I never knew, were shot in front of her.

With his success, my father bought one of the first cars in the Eastern Cape, a Hupmobile. Ironically, it was the automobile that killed his ostrich business. The large, feather-adorned hats wouldn't fit into a saloon car, and boas and hats would fly off in an open one. The collapse of the ostrich market was a financial disaster, but my father devised an irrigation system and turned his dry Karoo properties into sheep farms. The best farm was in Somerset East, where he had gone to live. Then the wool market collapsed in the Depression of the 1930s. After that he ran a small hotel in Dordrecht, a village in the Eastern Cape, though this clearly had no great future. He then began to barter blankets for skins, hides, and grain in nearby Basutoland. Blankets were worn as a sort of warm cape by the Basuto. He would take pony trains loaded with blankets up into the Drakensberg, a formidable mountain escarpment that separates the coastal plains from the veld of the high interior plateau, and come back loaded with hides and grain. With the proceeds of this trading he bought a hotel and trading store in Cedarville, in what was then East Griqualand. It was during this period that he courted, then married Rachel Zepporah Werner, whose family lived in Piet Retief in the Eastern Transvaal, a town larger than Cedarville. Cedarville was undeniably a *dorp*, a derogatory Afrikaans term for a small, unimportant village.

My mother never liked Cedarville. She hated its parochialism and had few friends in the district. My parents decided that Cedarville wasn't the best place to bring up a Jewish child, and in 1935 they sold everything and moved to the east-coast city of Durban, in the Province of Natal. It was a courageous move, especially since South Africa was hit particularly hard by the Depression. Durban lies in a subtropical zone, with a lush and fertile coast. The city was established in the nineteenth century by the British and their agent Sir Benjamin d'Urban. It had been a thriving Indian Ocean port, both an industrial and tourist city, but the Depression had taken a toll.

My father looked for a new enterprise. As he was familiar with running a hotel and bottle stores, he conducted a form of market research by following the trucks that delivered beer from the two local breweries — the Castle and the Lion — and chatting with their drivers. Eventually, he discovered a hotel in the suburb of Bellair with a bar and bottle store that was moving large volumes of beer, but didn't appear to be prospering. The Bellair Hotel was owned by two Irishmen, the Bisset brothers. Located on the old mainline, it had a substantial blue-collar and East Indian (mostly Hindu) population. The Bisset brothers made their own substantial contribution to the consumption of alcohol, which explained the poor profits. They were happy to lease the hotel to my parents — why work when you could make as much without working? My father insisted on a long lease, which was just fine with the Bissets.

With very hard work and careful control, the hotel, bar, and bottle store began to produce a substantial income. After the fall of Singapore in 1942, Durban had the only dry dock capable of repairing troop ships and warships on the Indian Ocean: the city prospered. The Bellair Hotel had an open-air dance floor, laid out around a giant ficus tree, and it became a popular place for soldiers, sailors, and airmen heading to India and Egypt. It was the big-band era: the sounds of Benny Goodman and Glenn Miller wafted through the evening air.

At first my mother directed the catering side of the hotel, and, when necessary, acted as housekeeper. My father worked as a barman when things got busy. They simply did what was necessary to make the business a success. When the hotel eventually came up for sale my parents were in a position of advantage, with their long lease, to buy the property. This was followed by the purchase of the Malvern Hotel further up the main line. They also began to accumulate underdeveloped industrial sites around the city. As a consequence, I grew up with a strong sense of material security.

The nursery school I attended was idyllic. Joyce Borden, the daughter of our local senator, ran the school in her house. It was one of the early houses of Natal, built in high Victorian colonial style: wide verandahs with cast-iron posts, multicoloured tile floors, rooms with high pressed-metal ceilings that opened onto verandahs with French windows and louvred mahogany shutters.

School was conducted under the leafy umbrella of a bulbous ficus tree. A blackboard stood on an easel under the tree. When it rained, we used the billiard room, with its ornate clerestory and conical green-shaded lamps hung low over the billiard table. The sunken garden, with its pools, lily ponds, and grottos, was the stage for the annual pantomime. I have a picture of myself from one performance, dressed as a pixie.

Two great iron gates on stone posts marked the entrance to the drive. We used to swing on these — or rather, to sail. One we named the Queen Elizabeth, the other the Queen Mary. Senator Borden, if he drove by, would stop and we would hitch a ride in the dickey seat of his stylish coupe. Joyce Borden had a brother who had his own airplane, and he once flew over the house and dropped a bag of candies for us on the tennis court. Tragically, he was killed in a plane crash not long after. Joyce never married. She took to drinking as she grew older, and had an affair with the local doctor, Dr. Sacks. When I went to Oxford she went out of her way to tell me how gratified she was, but she said it with some surprise, I think.

Tom, our gardener, was a Zulu with a beard and lively eyes, dark, tall, and angular. He conjured snakes out of our garden. He would place the flat of a spade on the snake so just its head showed, dangle the open mouth of an jute sack in front of it, then lift the spade. The snake would make a lunge into the bag and the trap shut.

Whenever Tom needed extra money, he presented one of these writhing snake bags to my mother. She would take it to Fitzsimmons Snake Park, where they paid two shillings a foot for snakes. They used the poison to create a serum. Just before he disappeared from our lives, Tom caught a fourteen-foot black mamba in the grenadilla bush. It was too big for the bag, and Tom had his picture in the paper holding the mamba at one end on a spade, and on the other end a rake, to accommodate its length.

The grenadilla bush was where we children had played house. After that, we needed a new place. With Tom gone we also needed a new gardener. Peter came: a safe man, dull and plodding. He had lost one eye — I never found out how. He had the flattest feet I'd ever seen, the soles cracked at the edges.

Samson, a Zulu with a short temper, was my parents' cook for forty years. His *milchika kneidlach*, *tzimmes*, and *lokshen kugel* were excellent. On university vacation, when I slept in, I would be woken by Samson, ostensibly feeding our dogs outside my bedroom door, telling them to "Jump up. Time for breakfast."

Both Harry Meyers and the Lazars, my father's relatives, lived in Pretoria, and it was arranged that I would visit them. I must have been about ten at the time. Harry and Doreen lived in a flat below the Union building (which was designed by Herbert Baker, Lutyens's rival imperial architect), as did Harry, Milly, and Nathan Lazar. Together they operated a highly successful jewellery store.

The Lazars' house was Victorian, on a corner site. The garden was filled with tropical plants and the muffled drip of an artificial bird bath fountain, flanked by a deep, multicoloured, tile-floored, cast-iron-columned verandah. Each evening the three of them met on the verandah for a sundowner before dinner. Dinner was prepared by their butler/cook, a Black man from central casting. He was tall, white-haired, and with an aristocratic bearing: his pantry was filled with glass jars filled with peaches and pears he had preserved.

The house had an extraordinary silence, broken only by the *tick tock* of the grandfather clock that sat on the broad landing of the crimson-carpeted stair to the second floor. Its hourly chimes and the audible marking of seconds only seemed to emphasize the quiet of the house.

Harry was a bachelor, a man of heavy features and low, gravelly voice. He wore a gold chain necklace and a weighty gold jewelled wrist watch. I noted a bedside radio, unusual for the time. Each July he spent two weeks at the King Edward hotel, Durban's poshest, to coincide with the July Handicap, a sort of Ascot horse race, and then the Gold Cup, an equally social and horsey event. It was only much later that I worked out he must have been gay.

Milly resembled him, but always coifed her artificially blond hair to perfection. Her husband Nathan could not have been in greater contrast to Harry: a high-pitched voice; darting, unconfident gaze; and abstemious dress.

There were other Lazars in Pretoria. One morning I was picked up by a charming woman, who walked me down to her house where I met her son, who must have been in his twenties. At university he had switched from engineering to medicine. He made me the perfect present: a balsa model of a Spitfire fighter plane, small enough to fit in the palm of my hand. The undercarriage was made from two pins, the heads acting as wheels.

While in Pretoria I asked to/insisted on visiting the house of Paul Kruger, the exiled president of the short-lived Transvaal Republic. Its modesty spoke of his lack of pretension and his simple Dutch Reform faith. Indeed, he still believed the earth to be flat.

After the stay in Pretoria I took the train to Johannesburg to meet my father, who had timed a business trip to drive me back to Bellair.

. . .

My parents' cultures differed widely, despite their devotion to one another. My father dedicated his energies to making a success of whatever enterprise he was engaged in, working up to eighteen hours a day if required. My mother grew up in South

Africa where servants did the menial work and had time for sports — golf, tennis, and horseback riding. She was a natural athlete, and I still have her golf trophies. Since my father rarely left the business, my mother, sister, and I, when not vacationing in Piet Retief, would head to the Drakensberg, to walk and climb or play golf.

It was in Harrismith in the Orange Free State, on a golfing holiday, at about the age of twelve, that I was approached by an African employee of the hotel in which we were staying. He asked me if there was a position for him in our hotel in Bellair, a suburb of Durban. I have no idea how he knew of our hotel there. Without much thought, I must have given him some intimation that there was such a possibility.

I thought no more about it until Phineas, the young African, to my great surprise and even greater consternation, turned up in Bellair. He must have walked most, if not all, of the three hundred kilometres between the two cities. With great trepidation I told my mother of the situation. Fortunately for me, she gave him employment.

Months later a member of the hotel staff told me that Phineas was very ill. I went to the hotel's staff quarters, and found Phineas lying on his stomach, his mother sitting beside him in silent vigil. She peeled back the bed cover to reveal a horrendous wound in Phineas' buttock. It must have been a half inch deep and four inches square.

I immediately told my mother, who had Phineas admitted to the King Edward hospital, the hospital that had unaccountably discharged Phineas a week earlier. Septicemia of the wound by this time had progressed too far, and Phineas died soon after admission. This episode has haunted me ever since. I often think of him when I wake at night, and still mourn his death.

. . .

Because of my mother's attachment to her family and the hot, humid summer on the coast (there were very few buildings with air conditioning then), we spent prolonged periods in Piet Retief. Summers there on the high veld were hot, but dry.

I remember the train journey from Durban to Piet Retief, the coziness of the compartment, lying in the fresh-smelling bunk with clean sheets and coarse blankets. From the top bunk I could slide open a small panel and look into the corridor. When the train stopped at night, I looked through the panel to the lights of the deserted station and sleeping town. The only sounds were of railway men talking to each other in Afrikaans as they approached, swinging their coffee cans, coughing in the night chill. I could see the vapour of their breath.

We woke to a countryside that was rolling veld — brown grassland — a contrast to the lush, wet coastal plain we'd left. The steward who brought breakfast had a master key to open the sliding door. He was supposed to knock and wait, but his wait was never long. My mother suspected he opened up quickly to get a glimpse of ladies in some stage of undress.

At Volksrust we changed engines, as the line was electrified only so far, and were attached to two coal-burning locomotives. The train stopped at places that couldn't be called stations, although they had wonderful names in black railway lettering on whitewashed boards. There would be a water tank and a few wattle trees. A group of African women huddled beneath the trees, staring blankly at the train with silent babies strapped to their backs. You seldom heard African children cry. The older children, often naked, would beg at the side of the train. Other than the children's voices, the silence was supreme; it sang in your ears. The *ku-kurru*-ing of doves in the wattle trees emphasized the desolate sense of the place. When the train left, the wayside stop would have no definition at all, though the Africans, in their bright prints, with their brass-studded, gaily painted wooden trunks and their blanket rolls, would sit there still.

The train wound slowly among boulder-strewn *kopjes* (flat-top hills), the rocks glinting with heat in the sun. The sky was terribly high, and the thick white clouds huge, their grey under-bellies hovering monumentally over the land. At last we reached Piet Retief. My mother's family had all lived in this small town, named for one of the leaders of the Great Trek of 1834. My grandfather still lived there, although my grandmother was long dead. My aunt and uncle also lived there, and, depending on whether my aunt was talking to her sister-in-law at that point or not, we would be met by both families at the station.

My first impression was the smell of the fine dust. Their car, a Ford colloquially known as a Tin Lizzie, was kept carefully, but the dust still managed to get into the seams of the stitched seats. The car was stifling in the mid-day heat and the windows had turned yellow from exposure to the sun.

My maternal grandfather, Jacob Werner, son of Rabbi Aba Werner, had immigrated from London to South Africa in the early 1890's. At first he had a job as a clerk in a dry goods store in Vryheid, a small town in Natal near the border of Transvaal. He married Rebecca Abrams-Levy of Glasgow and they moved to the eastern Transvaal before the outbreak of the Anglo-Boer War. They travelled for the last leg of the journey in an ox cart, as the railway at that time hadn't reached so far into the interior. "Oom Jacob" (literally, *Oom* means "Uncle," but it is used as a general term of respect by Afrikaaners), either bought or built the Imperial Hotel, eventually became mayor of Piet

Retief, and master of the local Masonic Lodge. Astronomy was his passion, and he built his own observatory. He provided the local meteorological report, and became a fellow of the Royal Astronomical Society for a rather slender thesis on sundials. This would seem to indicate a man of great energy, but I suspect it was really vanity and self-importance. It was my grandmother, his Glaswegian wife, who built their house, bore four children, and managed the family.

At the centre of town was an arid square with a water pump. Both Dutch Reformed and Lutheran churches were not far from the square. Covered ox wagons were periodically camped there, the farmers coming in for *Nachtmaal*, or communion. On the other side of the square were the city hall and a general store owned by an Indian merchant. Sacks of grains, with their tops rolled down to display the merchandise, lined the entrance to the store. It was redolent with the smells of grains, spices, and large, coarse bars of yellow soap like fresh-cut lumber stacked to cure.

The Imperial Hotel was an imposing structure with a double-storey cast-iron balcony across its front. Jacob's second son, Bernard, assisted him in running it, though it wasn't clear how much help he was. Bernard had acquired great billiards skills and was an excellent golfer, given more to leisure than to work.

Behind the hotel was a low barn with long trestle tables inside. Commercial travellers who stayed at the hotel used the barn to display their wares. Behind it was an iron gate that opened to a small garden that contained Zaida's (*Zaida* is "grandfather" in Hebrew) round observatory with its rollaway, hemispherical roof and brass telescope. One entered the family house through the back door — the formal front entrance, never used, faced onto the street on the other side of the house. Further up the street was the town's modest brick synagogue, in which my parents were married.

I would play with my cousins in the Werner garden, an expanse of bare ground that had a slight roll. We made roads, bridges, kraals (animal enclosures), barns, and buildings. We drove small toy cars and trucks on the roads and over bridges that were either cut into the ground or built up, as the contours required. We ran a hose into a small depression to make a river. It was a self-contained world of our making, and lasted for weeks, with inspired additions, becoming far more than we could have imagined when we started.

When in Piet Retief my mother, my sister, and I stayed with Ettie and George Susser, my mother's sister and brother-in-law. I think it was only once that my father accompanied us — he was never happy being away from his business.

In the Sussers' yard was a locquat tree we climbed to tell stories. There was an odd structure containing the toilet which supported a circular corrugated-iron water tank above. Water for the tank was pumped up by an iron pump with a long handle. A man came and performed this arduous exercise each morning. The toilet was not water-flushed, however; a night-soil cart would remove the creosoted buckets before we awoke.

An early morning sound was the ring of iron on the blacksmith's forge across the road.

Selina was the laundry maid. She did the washing in a galvanized bathtub with a corrugated washing board in the yard outside the kitchen. A shy African, she wore blue and white dotted clothes with a large folded headdress of the same material as her dress. I was never sure if she was Swazi or Basuto.

There was a three-legged iron pot outside where a coarse corn-meal was worked to make *putu*. This was done by hand, working the dough into a shape the size and texture of a hand grenade, which was then dipped in sugar or salt. I often joined the staff to eat putu.

There were other Jewish families in the town. The Mezrachs owned a tobacco factory. It had a tall, thin metal chimney that puffed rhythmically, and a steam hooter to mark shifts. The concrete courtyard between the corrugated iron industrial buildings was perfect for roller skating, although only one skate could ever be found for me.

The Jaffes owned a soft drink bottling plant. Mr. Jaffe, a kindly gentleman with an equally sweet-natured wife, had no children, and indulged my cousins and me — we often visited them to be given soft drinks taken off the bottling belt before they were capped. Dr. Baron, the town's doctor, was Jewish, as well.

The other family I remember were the Lapiduses. They weren't prosperous, and Mr. Lapidus spent long periods in Portuguese East Africa in some mysterious occupation. But the daughter, much older than myself, was a dark beauty and I secretly fell in love with her. The Lapiduses disappeared, and I don't know what became of them. Mr. Lapidus, I think, died in odd circumstances. We assumed it was suicide.

The trips to Piet Retief were wonderful, but going to school there, which the long sojourns required of me, wasn't. Lessons were conducted in Afrikaans, which was then almost unknown to me. And while I'd had to contend with anti-Semitism in the primary school in Bellair, here it was even worse. At home I was given much moral instruction about being proud of my Jewish heritage as a defence.

These were the war years, and South Africa was split between those who supported Britain and the Commonwealth, and those who opposed British interests. These were mostly Afrikaners, who nurtured the bitter legacy of the Anglo-Boer War, which had been particularly savage. Under Lord Roberts, the British had pursued scorched-earth tactics, imprisoning the wives and children of the Boer farmers who were away at war. The prisons were essentially concentration camps, and many of the women and children died of cholera. Notwithstanding the establishment of an independent Union of South Africa in 1910, the Boers felt they'd lost their country to the British, and, like the Irish, would join anyone fighting against them. And the racist doctrine and anti-Semitism of the ascendant Nazis dovetailed with the white supremacy found in South Africa.

The district surrounding Piet Retief staunchly supported the Nationale Party, the party of apartheid and white superiority; their sympathies were distinctly pro-Nazi. As the only Jewish boy in the school — my cousins in Piet Retief who attended school were girls — I came in for a great deal of abuse. I was surrounded each day by groups of tough farmers' children and taunted. My refuge lay in mentally composing great speeches, my oratory moving large audiences to my point of view, or engaging in debates where I would powerfully refute my adversary's argument.

While the area around Piet Retief was nationalist and pro-Nazi, the pro-British Union Party formed the government. It was led by General Smuts, a Boer general who became an ardent supporter of the British commonwealth. He strategically established a very large army training camp on the outskirts of Piet Retief, which brought both prosperity and conflict. I remember olive-drab army trucks pulling up to my uncle's liquor store to load up with cases of beer, wine, and spirits. Saturday mornings were busy. The customers were mostly soldiers but there was a farmer who was seven feet tall, one of a family of giants. When he stood at the counter I could still see the street through his legs.

On Saturday nights, the town hall had a weekly movie. Both soldiers from the camp and locals would be in the audience. Performances started with a rendition of "God Save the King," while his image was projected on the screen. Soldiers, and those supporting the South African war effort, loyally stood to attention. Those opposed to the war steadfastly remained in their seats. Fights broke out as soldiers attempted to pull them into standing positions.

Route marches were a regular feature of camp training. They started early in the morning and I remember being woken by the sound of crunching gravel as thousands of boots marched in step past our house. I crept to the window and pulled the blind aside to see an unending phalanx sway in time as it moved along. Occasionally they would sing.

General Smuts led successful campaigns in the First World War in the former German colonies of South West and East Africa. Louis Diamond, my father's brother, and Bernard Werner, my mother's brother, both served in the South African army — Louis in South West Africa and Bernard in East Africa. Louis received the sword of a captured German officer, which he subsequently gave me. He was invalided out with black water fever, but he survived.

Bernard served in an armoured car regiment. Armoured cars were not the heavy, well-protected vehicles they subsequently became: his was overturned by a rhino who took exception to the vehicle's presence in his territory. Bernard and crew spent the night up a tree until the rhino eventually ambled off.

On September 5, 1939, my mother and grandfather, Zaida, who was visiting us, tucked me in and wished me good night. "Russia has made a pact with Germany," Zaida said, then collapsed across the foot of my bed. He had had a massive stroke, and died instantly. I remember the coffin being loaded into the train's goods coach. My sister, Stella, and I accompanied my mother to Piet Retief for my grandfather to be buried next to Rebecca, his wife, in the Jewish cemetery there.

The most rapturous outings were trips taken to Peavaan, a simple resort nestled in a boulder-strewn river valley of hot sulphur-water springs. It was a three- or four-hour drive from Piet Retief. Having left before dawn we would stop at first light to have a roadside breakfast: lamb chops, warm buttered fresh rolls, and café au lait.

We would arrive before lunch, in time for a swim. The hotel was spartan — whitewashed plaster walls, the bedrooms, with iron bedsteads, arranged in a long building with access to the rooms from the wide veranda. The dining room and small shop were built amid huge boulders, the most unconventional setting for a building I had seen. The pools were reached via stone steps built between boulders. The best pools were natural rock pools; these were the hottest. They became progressively cooler and larger, the larger pools being man-made. Both *dassies* (rock rabbits) and humans sunned themselves on the pale tan rocks. Because the pools were tepid at their coolest, one could spend long periods playing in the water. Whether it was this, or some property of the sulphides in the water (it certainly was not the aroma), we were always ravenous by mealtimes. And the wholesome country food was delicious — oatmeal porridge, steak and eggs, and fresh bread for breakfast; cold meats, salads, and fruit for lunch; and thick stews for dinner.

There is a stillness to high veld afternoons, and the heat can be intense. C.J. Langenhoven, an early twentiety-century Afrikana poet, evokes the sense of it in his line *"selfs die wit-kraai soek die skade"* (even the white crows seek the shade). The adults took long afternoon naps, but as children we found it hard to sleep in the day. Once we were in a games room that had a ping-pong table and a sofa. A few of us jumped up and down on the sofa. I looked down and saw the yellow head of an enormous puff adder, one of Africa's deadliest snakes, poking out from below the sofa. I must have broken the long-jump record — I think I left the room in one bound. The hotel staff killed the snake with a *knobkerrie*, a long stick with a ball on the end. It was considered too dangerous to use a gun inside the building for fear of a ricocheting bullet.

Violent summer storms punctuated life in Piet Retief. Huge, black cumulonimbus clouds streaked with lightning, crashing thunder reverberating across the veld. There were often hailstorms, and the sound of hail on the corrugate iron roof was deafening. After the storm passed, the rain-soaked earth smelled sweet, intoxicatingly fresh, the land reborn.

We followed the course of the Second World War with intense interest. We had maps of the theatres of war, and would track with pins the retreat or advance of allied forces, particularly in North Africa. Members of the family had joined the Sixth Division, the South African component of Montgomery's Eighth Army in North Africa. There were posters everywhere: "Loose lips sink ships." This, at times, turned out to be literally true; two cousins who departed in a convoy bound for Egypt were reported on *Zeeson*, the Nazi propaganda radio, with details of their departure and the size of the convoy, causing their mother much worry, though both sons returned unscathed.

We were aware of the plight of European Jews, but we did not know the extent of their persecution. The horror of the camps had yet to be discovered. The situation of my father's family wasn't discussed. It was only after the war that we became aware of what had happened to them. My father made contact with Esther, his niece, via the Red Cross. She was in a displaced persons camp. She, her sister Masha, and Masha's daughter were the only members of the family to survive the Holocaust. Arrangements were made for Esther to live with us in South Africa, but that lasted only six months. She wanted to join a man she had met in the displaced persons camp who had emigrated to Israel. And she felt useless living an unproductive life.

Masha had left her very young child on the doorstep of a non-Jewish neighbour's house as she was being transported to a concentration camp. After the war she had difficulty reclaiming her: the foster parents were by then understandably reluctant to give her up.

Three

School Days in South Africa

LILY STEIN, WIFE OF PHILIP STEIN, A PROFESSOR OF MATH-
ematics at Natal University and parents of my friend Wilfrid,
persuaded my mother to enrol me at Durban High School
(DHS), whose culture was *mens sana in corpore sano* (a healthy
mind in a healthy body), instead of the high school favoured by
local children. The contrast between it and the primary school
could not have been greater. A welcome difference was the absence of overt anti-Semitism, though Jewish boys were clearly
identified: we stood outside the hall during morning prayers,
then filed in for the announcements. The culture was that of
an English public school. A dress code was firmly maintained:
flannels, blazer, and school tie — despite the humid summers
— and an optional straw "basher." There was a science stream

and a classics stream: a false dichotomy. To this day I regret missing Latin, as I chose the science stream. However, the physics, chemistry, and mathematics stood me in good stead later in the school of architecture.

One teacher had a profound effect on me. Bill Payne was my English teacher, a Mr. Chips writ large. He was well over six feet tall and had enlisted in the South African army in the Second World War. The army didn't have size fourteen boots to fit him, so he was paid an extra sixpence a day to get boots made to measure. He had been captured at Tobruk by Rommel and sent to a prisoner of war camp in Germany. He survived the notorious forced marches as the Allies advanced across France and Germany near the end of the war. This was during one of the coldest winters of the twentieth century. His boots were in tatters, and he avoided frostbite only by wrapping his feet in newspapers. It was his spirit and leadership that pulled his troops through.

On prize day, Bill was the only teacher not in cap and gown. Instead, he was in a light-brown tweed suit. His qualification was not a university degree, but a teaching certificate, awarded in a postwar course for veterans. He ran the marathon from Pietermaritzburg to Durban in rugby boots, stopped for a beer and steak halfway, and still finished under the required time. Still, it was his love of language that so thoroughly engaged me. We could spend a whole lesson on just three lines of Shakespeare. Bill criticized the use of the word *cavalcade* when describing a convoy of cars. He cited the Latin root word for cavalcade — *caballus*, a pack-horse. "There are no horses in a convoy of cars," he explained. "Please sir; horsepower, sir," I replied. My puns and such contributions accorded me his greatest praise: "Diamond, you foul boy."

Each master was expected to hold regular tests to establish class ranking, but Bill dispensed with that formality. The day before the test results were to be filed with the headmaster, Bill would line us up around the classroom walls. He had three coat check tabs, numbered 1, 2, and 3. Each pupil was asked three questions. For the boy who didn't get any answers correct he would ask what movie was on at the Roxy.

I am not exactly sure when I began to be called Jack instead of Abel. It must have been sometime between the third and fourth forms at DHS. Masters used only last names, so the origin must have been with school chums. There are two possible sources for this switch — at fifteen or sixteen I was taller than my father, whose name was Jacob, but he was called Jack, so my friends jokingly called me "little Jack." The other possible source was being called, again jokingly, "Jack of Diamonds." In any event the nickname stuck, much to my father's disapproval because of a clear difference between Ashkenazi and Sephardic traditions. Among the former, no one is ever named after a living relative; among the latter, names of children are frequently those of living relatives.

Between the third and fourth forms my life was transformed. I grew to over six feet but retained my running speed and excelled at sports. There are good reasons why the poor, the underprivileged, and the disenfranchised revere sports, and why there are sports heroes: success is achieved by prowess, not by birth, wealth, privilege, or subterfuge. There are rules, which, if not obeyed, lead to penalty. All are treated equally on the field of play. No one has an extraneous advantage.

Track and field and rugby gave me a self-confidence I hadn't achieved in any other way. It was life-changing, though it also led to rebellious behaviour in the classroom. I remember telling Mr. deKock, who gave a lesson about faith, that I didn't believe in God. He astonished me by saying. "Diamond, you are probably the most religious boy in the class."

. . .

To our great surprise, my classmate Donald Langford and I were given permission by our parents to hitchhike from Durban to Salisbury in Rhodesia (now Harare in Zimbabwe), a two-thousand-kilometre trip, during the 1948 winter vacation. We were sixteen.

The first leg of the journey, Durban to Johannesburg, was with an acquaintance returning to the Rand. We spent a few days with one of Donald's relatives — an orthopaedic surgeon whose son was a Springbok cricketer.

The next stretch was from Johannesburg to the Limpopo river. At dusk, we were picked up by an Afrikaner driving an ancient pickup truck, bound for Messina, close to the border between South Africa and Rhodesia. He suddenly veered off the road to chase a hare, which he shot, then calmly resumed the trip. He asked where we would sleep that night, and we said probably in the open. He told us that the Limpopo valley was rife with malaria-bearing mosquitoes and offered his screen-enclosed veranda for the night, which we gratefully accepted. The next morning, we walked across the Beit Bridge over the Limpopo, checking in with Rhodesian customs and immigration officials. Again, we were asked where we would sleep on our way to Bulawayo. Our non-committal reply triggered this response: "Don't sleep on the ground because the lions will get you, and don't sleep in the trees, as the leopards will."

Rhodesia was landlocked (as Zimbabwe still is) and all freight travels either by road or by rail. At the border there was a line of vehicles ready for departure into the country. I had a driver's licence I had acquired in Cape Town, using my uncle's car for the test, so I asked the person marshalling the group if they needed drivers. They did, we were assigned a car to drive, and our convoy headed out. In front of us, a man driving an MG with the top down was lulled to sleep in the sun and drove off the road, damaging the new vehicle. The convoy stopped at Que Que, and the leader of the group asked us to give up our vehicle to the discredited MG driver, which we did.

We had stopped at a small collection of rondavels (round, mud-wall buildings with conical thatched roofs). One of the rondavels was a pub. Inside, two stalwarts were drinking their morning beer, and one was an old DHS boy. They offered us a ride to Bulawayo. We perched in the back of their pickup, one on each side of a loosely tethered engine they were transporting. To conserve concrete during the war, roads consisted of two paved tracks, known as strip roads, rather than being fully paved. Over time the ground around the tracks had eroded, so the strips were higher than the ground. When traffic approached from the opposite direction, the vehicles each bumped over onto one track. The pickup truck we were in was ancient and routinely suffered punctures from the jagged edges of the concrete strips. It also broke down repeatedly. After each repair, quart beer bottles with screw tops were pulled out from beneath the seat, and there was a celebratory drink. I asked about the engine they were transporting. Once a year they took it from Que Que to Wankey, simply as an excuse for a road trip and an escape from their families.

In Bulawayo we stayed with a school chum and had the luxury of a hot shower and decent food. Sunsets in Rhodesia are extraordinary, covering the sky from horizon to horizon in crimson, corrugated clouds.

In the morning we went to the Bulawayo Bedford truck dealer and asked if they needed any vehicles delivered to Salisbury. They had a panel van that needed to be delivered, which we gladly took. This was 1948, and petrol (gas) rationing was still in effect, so we were given petrol coupons for the trip. Around midnight we were low on fuel and stopped at a petrol station in a small village. The night watchman explained that the pumps were locked, and we would need to get the keys from the owner.

The owner lived outside the town in a small shack with a low doorway. Inside the murky hut was a small hurricane lamp, exaggerating the horror of a man in an advanced stage of leprosy. I could see through the flesh to his skull. The hair on the back of my neck literally stood up. At sixteen, I had few resources to cope with this sight. I took the keys from him and was sure I'd contract leprosy myself. He instructed us to bring the keys back, but I left them with the night watchman.

Early the next morning we arrived at Salisbury to stay with my cousin Doreen and her husband Harry Meyers, a former army captain, and one of the best-looking men I have known. He came from Pretoria, and once drove me there from Piet Retief to stay with relatives of my father's. I was deeply impressed when he stopped to give an African a lift, unusual at that time.

Harry had fought in Eritrea and the Egyptian desert, and had brought back a magnificent wax painting, done by an Italian soldier, of a beautiful bust of an Ethiopian woman. The

Italians were routed in Eritrea, and I suppose this was one of the spoils of war. He and Doreen had been married in my parents' home in Durban. The reception was held in our rose garden, surrounded by royal palms. They had opened a bookstore in Salisbury. A few years later Harry inexplicably committed suicide, leaving Doreen with three children.

Four

University Life

THERE WERE NO ARCHITECTS IN MY FAMILY. I WAS THE first to receive a university degree of any kind. I am not sure why I applied to the School of Architecture at the University of Cape Town, rather than the closer Witwatersrand University in Johannesburg. Perhaps it was the attractiveness of the Western Cape and its Mediterranean climate, and my familiarity with Cape Town, having spent holidays there while visiting Uncle Louis and Aunt Annie Diamond.

Louis and Annie could charitably be called parsimonious. When they were both out of the house, they locked the phone to prevent the maid from using it. Calls cost a "tickey" then — the South African name for a three-penny coin. They would owe each other money for postage stamps. They drove across town to the wholesale market to buy bags of fruit and vegetables to save a few pennies, and I often wondered if they took into consideration the cost of petrol and the wear and tear on the car. The uneaten fresh fruit was bottled. There was no way all the accumulated food could have been consumed in their lifetimes. Perhaps Annie had an economic way of using rotting fruit.

Louis and a partner had established the Good Hope furniture factory in Salt River, an industrial suburb on the opposite side of the city from Sea Point. Their product was aimed at the lower end of the market. I visited the factory once and saw a workman using a spray gun, the kind used in car body repair shops, to cover a piece of furniture with varnish. This enterprise provided Louis with a substantial income.

Louis travelled each day by public transit to the factory; first by bus into the city, then by a suburban commuter train to Salt River, saving a few more pennies.

Their house on High Level Road in Sea Point, an attractive suburb of Cape Town on the lower slopes of Signal Hill, overlooked the Atlantic Ocean from the promontory that encloses Table Bay. It had a minuscule rear garden. Louis would wear dungarees, rubber boots, and gloves to garden. I never knew either fruit or vegetables, let alone flowers, to come from the garden.

I remember the rhythmic, mournful bleat of the foghorn when the Cape was enveloped in a thick, misty blanket; and the long copper hunting horn blown by the passing Cape Malay fishmongers from their two-wheeled, one-horse carts; and the call "Straw'bries! Straw'bries! Waaatermelon! Waaatermelon!" from fruit sellers on similar carts.

The rare combination of Beaux Arts and modernist architecture that shaped the academic and design curriculum of the school suited me perfectly. I had been a mediocre math student in high school, but suddenly calculus made sense, now that it had the practical application of solving structural problems. I revelled in precision drafting, freehand drawing, and watercolour rendering. I had always drawn. I made an imaginative leap to playing house by designing houses, and I drew cityscapes and still lifes. That gave me a head start in the first year.

Louis Diamond had promised his two nephews a car if they matriculated with first-class passes. To my father's disgust Uncle Louis failed to keep his promise. My father then promised that if I did well in my first year at university, he would provide a car. He was good as his word, and I was given a gunmetal grey Citroën with red leather seats. During vacation, I could now *drive* the 1,500-kilometre trip from Durban to Cape Town, in two days, with a stop in Colesberg to stay with the parents of a fellow UCT student — "Pannie" Garlake.

Colesberg, in the Great Karoo, a semi-desert region of South Africa, was established by the Dutch East India Company. The Garlakes' house was once the VOC (*Vereenigde Oost-Indische Compagnie*, United East India Company) agents' house. I was always given the privilege of the gunroom in which to sleep. Ella Garlake was the perfect chatelaine, an island of civility and taste. The polished mahogany table, furnished with silver Georgian cutlery and candelabra, was the setting for exquisite cuisine, all somehow enhanced by being in this small town in the Karoo.

Colesburg was remote from the large cities, so newspapers took several days to arrive. One was therefore especially welcomed if one brought the morning editions of the *Natal Mercury* or the *Cape Times*, depending on the direction one was travelling. Jack Garlake was a lawyer and auctioneer, and while conducting auctions he would drink whisky camouflaged with milk. Alcohol wasn't something the staunch Dutch Reform farmers approved of. Long after I graduated, Jack was shot by a local sheep farmer. I never learned the motive for his murder.

My second year at UCT was a struggle. I had been coasting, and hadn't developed beyond my native capabilities. At times it was hard to even get up in the morning. I had trouble mastering the new academic material and the magnificent potential of architecture. It became clear that everyone had caught up to me, and had passed me, and now I had to catch up to them. That was the only year in the five-and-a-half year academic program that I did not receive the class prize. However, it was an important academic and organizational lesson.

After the second year, my energy returned, and I became a member of the university first teams in rugby and athletics. I was elected to the Student Representative Council (SRC), and became involved in South African politics. In 1953 we attempted to integrate the university swimming pool — excepting only the academic program, apartheid applied to every other aspect of non-white students' lives at UCT. Informers at the university reported our activities to the government and police, and we were put on the political police's list. Subsequently, one of our number, Albi Sachs, was jailed and held in solitary confinement.

Unlike in North America, there was no tradition of summer jobs for the then largely white student body in South Africa. There are two reasons for this: summer and winter vacations are relatively short, with somewhat shorter Easter and Michaelmas breaks. And as there was, and regrettably still is, a large underemployed African population, there was little need to hire students. However, at the end of my first year of architecture school I applied for a position as an apprentice bricklayer with a large construction company during the Christmas summer vacation. I wanted to find out how projects were actually managed and what was required for their successful construction.

I was assigned to a mid-rise apartment tower whose concrete frame was completed. The site faced Esplanade Park, which runs the length of Durban Bay.

At one end of the bay is a bluff on which a large lighthouse was strategically sited. The bluff made a natural windbreak for the port at the entrance end of the bay, but no such protection was afforded the apartment tower at the other end of the bay. Each morning, I would park my new Citroën blocks from the construction site. I did not reveal that I was an architecture student, but did make the mistake of admitting I was able to read plans: I was promptly assigned to mark the location of all internal and external brick wall positions, and to lay the first course of bricks on the recently cast concrete floor slabs. There was a union rule that not more than six hundred bricks were to be laid by any bricklayer in a day. I was in no danger of breaking that rule.

At the end of the day I'd be grateful to be back at my parents' house to soak my aching back. So, at first, I was pleased when I was moved to the plasterer's section. They were working on a loosely-planked metal scaffold on the eleventh or twelfth floor. The technique was to hold a hod piled with mortar in one hand, gather some on a rectangular wooden trowel with the other, take a step or two back onto the loose plank platform along the external face of the brick wall, and hurl the plaster from the wood trowel with sufficient force to adhere it to the wall. Standing on loose planking eleven stories up in a strong wind didn't exactly produce a sense of security. I developed an alternate plastering technique, albeit less efficient, of standing close to the wall and pressing lumps of plaster against the wall with my hands.

The "brickies," as they were called, were crude, but I learned very important lessons that summer. One was to produce construction documents with as much clarity as possible. Not just the details regarding the installation of various systems, materials, and technologies, but also how the worker would be able to effect the installation.

During my second year of architecture school, I worked in the office of Hanson and Tomkin in Durban. They were practitioners of the modern movement, which was based on the work of Le Corbusier and, to a degree, on Mies van der Rohe. It was first introduced in South Africa by Rex Martienssen. His book, *The Idea of Space in Greek Architecture*, was seminal, and he influenced a generation of progressive architects. Hanson and Tomkin's left-leaning politics was also a draw for me. Their office was an exciting place to work, though I was mostly confined to window details. I was once given the job of designing free-standing lettering for an entrance canopy. I was given a tutorial on typefaces and how to secure them to the cantilevered concrete canopy. It made me aware of how little I knew of design implementation. That and my bricklaying experience introduced me to layers of design consideration previously unthought of.

Once, while driving from Durban to Cape Town, I stopped to pick up a hitchhiker outside Bloemfontein. He spoke Afrikaans as his English was poor. He saw an orange I had in the open glove compartment and asked if he could have it. I said yes, and he ate it, peel and all. It turned out he hadn't eaten in days. He'd been released from the Bloemfontein prison a few days earlier after serving a sentence for the attempted murder of his wife. He had been given money on his release but spent it all on tobacco, which he then threw over the prison wall for the inmates: half for the Black section of the prison, half for the white. "*Swart en wit is deselvde in die tronk*" (Black and white are equal in jail), he said. I asked where he was heading. Back to his wife, he said. I hoped it would be a reconciliation.

. . .

For my thesis subject, I chose acoustics and the design of a concert hall, a perfect vehicle to indulge my two passions — architecture and music. By good fortune, the visiting lecturer that year was Philip Hope Bagenal, a prominent English acoustician. He become not only my thesis supervisor, but a wonderful mentor, as well. I learned much from him. There was a reason for the success of traditional concert halls and opera houses — their empirical development of shape, materials, and details produced wonderful acoustics — but they didn't look functional in the modern sense. The irony is that modernist shapes — particularly the fan-shaped auditorium — were exactly the opposite of what is required. Sound decays as it moves away from its source, so it needs reinforcing if the sound is to be equal for all locations in the hall. The fan shape, which widens as it moves away from the sound source, reduces the intensity of sound reflection. Those halls look functional, but they are decidedly not.

The Bachelor of Architecture degree at UCT required the fourth year of the degree program to be an internship in an architectural firm. This could be done anywhere in the world, provided it was in an accredited office. I chose London.

Professor Thornton White, the head of the University of Cape Town School of Architecture, provided a letter of introduction to the head of the Architectural Association, of which he was a graduate, and I was referred to the firm of Casson and Condor. Sir Hugh Casson had achieved great success as the architect of the Festival of Britain in 1951. Besides being an exhibition of note, it boosted the morale of a country still battered by the Second World War. Casson was a friend of the British royal family and designed the interior of their yacht, *Britannia*. My first task was designing a bar with a battleship-linoleum counter for the royal yacht.

In 1954, the journey from Cape Town to Southampton on the Union-Castle Line took two weeks. A classmate, who had arrived in London a month earlier, met me at Waterloo station on a Saturday afternoon in November. Fog shrouded London. We had lunch in a pub and went straight to the Albert Hall to hear a performance of Handel's *Messiah*. Sir Thomas Beecham was the conductor. The lamps on the stairs were still gas lamps. London was at the end of an era, not much changed from pre–Second World War days. I had never before left southern Africa, but this was all familiar to me. From nursery rhymes and books at school, I knew English and Commonwealth literature and history. Under Africa's sun, I had read of English fog and English glory. I had read Dickens, Conan Doyle, and Lytton Strachey, with his devastating satire of Prince Albert and the Albert Memorial. I was a part of the British Commonwealth. In travelling to its metropolitan heart, I was in some way coming home. Nothing in London was strange to me, and yet nothing was completely real. A magic realism perhaps. A heightened sense of London's essence, an atmosphere created by soft light and rain and the soot-blackened buildings.

Casson Condor's office was in what had been a house on the Old Brompton Road. As in most English buildings the heating was far from adequate. It was mostly supplied by a small gas fireplace. As I was a junior, lived nearby and was an early riser, it was my job to be first to arrive at the office and to light the gas fires. The office was conveniently near The Denmark, a pub. Our salary was paid weekly on Fridays, so Friday lunch was a half pint of bitter, and roast beef and two veg at the pub. A welcome change from pasta, or very cheap and not very good Chinese or Indian food.

There were far fewer foreign students in London then than there are now. The Colonial Office made every effort to welcome students from the British Commonwealth and to introduce us to events, personalities, and institutions of personal and professional interest. One such event was an invitation to a home in Chelsea, to a reception for Chagal. There was, however, a purpose more than merely social: our hostess wanted Chagal to assess the work of a young painter. I overheard her ask Chagal, after he was shown the artist's work, whether the young painter should continue to paint. Chagal's answer was that that decision must be entirely up to her. A Solomonic judgment, I thought.

The best part of London was that I had my own flat, in a courtyard in South Kensington. The anonymity of the city, the independence I felt there, sketch book and watercolours in hand, was sublime. After a concert in the Festival Hall I stood on Hungerford footbridge looking out at the Thames with a sense of exhilaration — I felt I could fly, or conquer the world. Anything was within my powers.

I bought a decommissioned 1938 taxi cab for twenty-five pounds and with friends I toured the south coast of England.

Then I sold the taxi and bought a Lambretta motor scooter. Together with a classmate, Owen Dolby, I travelled to Helsinki to visit my relatives — the Strachevskys. The visit concluded with a stay at their summer house on an island north of the city, an idyllic clapboard house with four-poster beds, feather-filled mattresses, and a sauna on the lake's edge. One of the family had been Sibelius's conductor, another an opera singer, and a third was a nurse who had served in a German field hospital when Finland was allied with Nazi Germany: an anomalous situation for a Jew, to say the least.

During the summer of 1954 I returned to South Africa. It was earlier than expected, because of a breakup with a girl-friend. My father asked me what I intended to do. I replied that I was deciding whether to find a place in an architect's office in Durban or in Cape Town. He said that if I left home and went to Cape Town he would not support me. I replied that he had just made up my mind, and that I was going to Cape Town. Within an hour I was on the road driving to the Cape.

It was a critical moment of independence. I felt a surge of exhilaration at the freedom and self-reliance it entailed. I found a place in an architect's office in Cape Town, and never looked back. To do my father justice, he did say that he thought I was wrong, but admired me for doing what I had decided. Perhaps the first compliment he ever paid me.

In 1956, my final year at UCT, a combined University of Cape Town and Stellenbosch University rugby team was selected for a European tour. We played against Italy, France, and Wales. Dr. Wells, the UCT rugby team doctor, and Dr. Atkins, of Guys hospital in London, arranged the British portion of our tour. We visited the Houses of Parliament, and as we entered the building, Dr. Atkins said to me, "Now Diamond, as an architect, I'm sure you will be interested in the Perpendicular style of the Gothic Revival Architecture of the building."

I was astonished that he would know that I was an architecture student, and even more astonished that he knew the names and academic courses of every member of the team. I learned a lesson in real politesse that day, something that was not prevalent in South African culture.

We lunched in Mansion House, in which there are plaques with the names of those British soldiers who fell in wars abroad. This included one devoted to those who fell in the Anglo-Boer war. A man from Stellenbosch University who was on the team, looked at the list of names on the plaque, and commented, "Not enough." This showed me, as nothing else in South Africa had, the depth and perpetuation of feeling, even two generations after the war.

That night we were given a dinner at which I was seated next to Brendan Bracken, Churchill's parliamentary private secretary during the Second World War. I could not have had a more fascinating and engaging dinner partner. My interest in history in general, and the Second World War in particular, was great, though at the time I had limited knowledge of the heroic role played by Churchill.

In the U.K. we visited Oxford and I looked up a UCT colleague, who encouraged me to apply to Oxford myself. We visited three colleges, and settled on University College, the oldest. My meeting with the dean consisted of a conversation about what was important to me, what ambitions I had, and what my academic record was. My average grades were in the A-range, with the class prize four years out of the five-year course, and the award of the rare Bachelor of Architecture with Distinction. I was nonetheless surprised to be accepted.

I sent a telegram to my parents telling them that I had been accepted by University College, Oxford, and asked if they would support me on this. I received an immediate positive reply. Their support for education, which they had not enjoyed themselves, was unreserved. However, I was never provided with funds beyond those required for tuition and a modest cost of living.

. . .

To get to Oxford, I flew from South Africa to Europe with Max, who was a pilot in a small start-up airline — Trek Airways. Its fleet consisted of three Vickers Viking planes. The fares, like the size of the fleet, were modest. Max had been a fighter pilot in Hermann Goering's "circus" in the First World War, but by 1938 the fate of Jews in Germany was clear to all except those who would not see. As a Jewish comrade-in-arms, Goering arranged for Max's exit, and Max ended up in South Africa where he was promptly interned as a German at the outbreak of war. After it was discovered that he'd been an ace fighter pilot, he was put to work training pilots in the South African Air Force.

After the war, Trek Airways was formed but hadn't secured landing rights in South Africa or Great Britain, nor were they licensed to fly at night. I took a train from Johannesburg to Lourenço Marques in Portuguese East Africa (now Maputo in Mozambique), the southern terminus of Trek Airways.

Our first night was spent in Entebbe. On the way there I asked Max if he would fly at a lower altitude so we could get a closer look at the plains teeming with game, but he declined. He had never had an accident, and said most accidents were due to pilot error and doing something unnecessary.

Flying over Khartoum the next day, the confluence of the Blue and White Niles (neither blue nor white, rather a muddy green) was clearly visible, and the dusty, monochromatic city was almost indistinguishable from the surrounding desert.

On arriving at Mersa Matruh on the Mediterranean coast of Egypt, some fifty miles from Cairo, and the furthest Rommel's Afrika Korps had advanced in North Africa in the Second World War, Max spotted an unusual aircraft parked at the end of the runway. After checking in at the hotel, he asked if I'd like to go back to the airport to take a look at this plane. It was guarded by two unkempt sentries armed with machine pistols. We were hustled into a small office and aggressively interrogated by an officer. At length we were allowed to go. On returning to the hotel, we found our rooms ransacked and our passports confiscated.

Missing a cashmere sweater but with passports handed back, we took off for Nice the next morning with great relief. It turned out the aircraft of interest was a Russian MiG, previously unseen in the West. Ten days after we left Egypt, the combined British, French, and Israeli forces invaded Nasser's Egypt in an abortive attempt to take over the Suez Canal. British, French, and other resident aliens were promptly incarcerated and spent the next two years in Egyptian prisons.

The last leg of the journey was from Nice to Dusseldorf, Trek Airways' northern terminus. It had taken two days to cross Africa's vast expanse, and little more than half a day (including a change of aircraft), to cross Europe. I took a British charter from Dusseldorf to London, and arrived, finally, at Oxford.

• • •

I had rooms overlooking Merton College gardens, and shared a living room with Nixon, a clarinet player. He spoiled my enjoyment of the Mozart clarinet concerto forever, practising regularly, loudly, and imperfectly. We also shared Archie, a manservant known as a "scout," who had a penchant for my sherry. My bedroom was poorly heated, and in the morning I would read in bed with gloves on. The warmest place in the college was the basement bathhouse. There were several large baths scattered around the room and each had a wood "bridge" on which to prop a book or a tankard of beer. I spent many happy afternoons there.

I was a member of the Centipedes, the Oxford athletic team. My races were the 100- and 220-yard sprints and long jump. I ran the 100 in 9.9 seconds (world record was 9.3 seconds) and this speed helped with rugby. Notwithstanding my history of playing for the University of Cape Town's first team, and being a member of the European tour, and being invited to the Springbok rugby trials for an Australia tour (I couldn't participate because of a broken bone in my foot), I was playing on the Greyhounds, essentially Oxford's second team. But their right wing — my position — was injured in the match before a scheduled Oxford–Wallabies (the touring Australian national team) match. I filled in, scored two tries, and we defeated the Australians. The first try was a short run to score, but the second was a fifty-yard run that involved handing off my opposing wing and sidestepping the fullback. Toft, the sports writer for the *Observer*, wrote that I must have been the best three-quarter reserve in the U.K. I was then included in the Blues team to play Cambridge. We were the underdogs. Toft said he would eat his hat if Oxford won. We did, and I was all for sending him a hat, but my teammates dissuaded me.

My rugby success was given some prominence via the local South African press. When my father heard, he wrote to me saying that he understood that I was still playing rugby. He said that "at my age I should get serious, instead of wasting time on games." He'd never seen me on a sports field. My father's childhood in a Jewish household in Lithuania and the need for self-reliance in South Africa had left no place for games. My mother had an appreciation for sport; she was an excellent golfer, tennis player, and equestrian. She was the one who encouraged my athletic activity.

My rugby success didn't extend to rowing, however. Eight members of our rugby team volunteered to form a crew to compete in the Eights Week event. Few of the eight had much rowing experience. I had none. Eights Week is an annual inter-college boat race. Boats are lined up along the banks of the Thames (known at Oxford as the Isis) River, about fifty metres apart in the order established the previous year. The object of the race is to touch the boat ahead. If successful, the positions are exchanged for the following day's race. The boat in first place, deemed Head of the River, is ceremonially burned in the victorious college's court.

There was no danger of that being us. We began practising three weeks before the event. Once we had the rudiments of oar action mastered, and a reasonable amount of coordination, the thrill of moving down the river on still mornings, the only sound the liquid slap of oars entering the water, and the subsequent surge of the boat, was compensation enough for our participation. A truly wonderful Oxford tradition, though we were never a threat to win. In one race the following boat bumped us so hard it knocked our cox into the river.

Each college had a barge moored to the bank of the river, literally the rowing club's boathouse. These barges, most of

them double-deckers, were crowded with fashionable onlook-
ers, many of whom were young women clad in their light summer finery.

. . .

I was impressed that there were no initiation rituals at Oxford.
Hazing is a barbarous, immature North American practice that
says as much about the administrators of those humiliations
as the humiliated. I was impressed with the dining protocols
at Oxford: gowns were worn, and a Latin grace delivered by a
classical scholar before meals. One could order beer or wine
from the butler and the Buttery supplied picnic hampers. The
College owned punts, which one could pick up at the base of
Magdalen's tower. Each college had a dining society with its
own wine cellar and silver, collected over the centuries.

I was surprised that the only mandatory academic requirement was the weekly, or perhaps biweekly, tutorial. At my first
tutorial I was assigned an essay and given a helpful bibliography
to read. I read the books and wrote the essay, assuming I had
done a good job of exhibiting my knowledge of the subject. I
read the essay to the tutor, who said, "Diamond, I know all
that. But what do *you* think?" A critical facility is at least as
important as knowledge: perhaps the best thing I learned at
Oxford.

Lectures by prominent faculty were given, often in the
dining hall of a college, but it was entirely up to the student
(always called an undergraduate) whether or not to attend.
Professor Wind, a German scholar, gave talks on art that were
so popular his lectures had to be given in the local cinema. The
subjects of the lectures I attended were Botticelli and Picasso.

He would stride onto the stage, lights off, and proceed without notes in cohesive, faultless sentences, delivered in his German accent. His insights have stayed with me, though some were of such complexity that I wondered whether they involved something intended by the artist or something invented by Wind.

. . .

That first summer, an Oxford friend — Neil Huxter, another South African — and I decided to spend the summer vacation in Rome, as travelling back to South Africa was out of the question. I managed to get a job with an English expat architect who lived in Rome, and whose practice was mostly in the Middle East — in Mosaddegh's Iran.

We arrived in Rome with no place to stay. The *Rome Daily American*, however, had a list of apartments for rent. One was a vast apartment in a relatively new building in a good area, Monti Parioli. The tenants were Americans who were going back to the United States for the summer. Italian law stated that one cannot get rid of a tenant if they choose not to go. Since we were clearly not going to stay after the summer, they accepted our paltry offer. In reality we were apartment-sitting.

King Farouk had the apartment below us — the Egyptian flag flew outside our balcony on Fridays. He never rose until noon, went out after dinner, and returned from the nightclubs in the early hours. We invited him to a party once, and while he never came, he sent up a tub of ice cream. Above us Fellini had the penthouse. His film *La Dolce Vita* was praised for its inventiveness, but all he had to do was turn his camera to the streets of Rome. The office where I worked was just off the Via Veneto, which was a Fellini scene each evening. Jane Mansfield almost caused a riot cruising by in her convertible wearing a low-cut dress.

An Italian undergraduate friend at University College had given me a letter of introduction to two families in Italy, one in Florence, the other in Rome. Neil and I travelled to Florence and presented our letter of introduction at what turned out to be the Palazzo Corsini. A footman took the letter while we waited in the loggia for an answer. He returned with an invitation to dinner. Dinner in a palace! Our expectations were high, so we had a light lunch.

Before dinner we had drinks on the garden terrace with the two Corsini daughters and the fiancé of one. Dinner was in a beautiful white and gold room, with footmen in attendance. A great silver tureen was wheeled in. However, the soup turned out to be the thinnest of consommés. After that course, Principessa Corsini made her entrance. We all stood up, the prince clicked his heels and bowed.

Another silver salver was brought in. To my dismay the main course appeared to be a few sardines. We thanked them for dinner and made our excuses to depart. Renata, one of the daughters, asked what we were going to do for the rest of the evening. I told her frankly that Neil and I were going to find a cafe that might have a fat hamburger. She asked if she could come, too.

The next day we were invited to accompany the family to the annual *Giuoco del Calcio Fiorentino*, an early, and very violent, form of football. The Corsini family were traditional heralds of the event, and we sat with them on the rostrum to review the participants, dressed in their brilliant medieval apparel, dipping their emblazoned banners as they passed the rostrum, and saluting the prince.

That night, we also accompanied them to witness the opening of the *Amerigo Vespucci* bridge over the Arno, destroyed by the Germans in the Second World War. We viewed the ceremony from the balcony of another Corsini palace, this one larger than the one the family inhabited. It was occupied by a football team. On our way through to the balcony we passed rows of foosball machines. Their incongruity was jarring.

In Rome we presented our other letter of introduction, this time with far less pomp and ceremony. We were invited to a cocktail party not far from our apartment building in Parioli. It was at this social event that I met Francesca Silver, who became a good friend. Her mother was appalled at this turn of events — I suspect her ambition for her daughter was to marry someone with an aristocratic title. She must have asked her husband to get rid of me. After dinner, Francesca's father asked me to have a chat in his study. He then invited me to accompany him to hunt boar on his estate in Sardinia. I told him I had a job in the city, and declined his invitation. I'm sure this gentle man told his battle-axe wife that he had really given me the gears. It reminded me of the Italian rendition of a fracas where one of the belligerents shouts "*Ti ammazzo*" (I'll kill you) but turns his head and whispers to supporters, "*Trattenetemi*" (hold me back).

Once it was clear that I was not going off to Sardinia, Francesca's mother had my family checked out in South Africa by the Italian ambassador. When Francesca discovered that, she chided her mother, saying, "*Non e gentile, mama.*"

Francesca subsequently married an engineer, a great person. We remained in touch, and years later, my wife Gillian and I stayed with them in Rome. When he was a young boy, our son Andrew spent a skiing holiday with them in Verbier. Francesca also visited us in Toronto.

In Rome, we would sometimes eat a picnic supper in the Forum — in 1956 there were no barriers and, in the evening, no tourists — not that there were many in the daytime. We sipped wine and ate *cichetti* on the stylobate of the Tholos; a still evening with a lapis lazuli sky, shot through with the sunset colours of Tiepolo. Even London, with its English predilection for domesticated grandeur, and L'Enfant's Washington fail to match Rome's splendour. It bestrides the world like a colossus.

Monks from various countries and dioceses rotate residence at Castel Gandolfo, the pope's summer residence outside Rome. Neil Huxter and I were in Rome during the time the Irish were in residence for the summer of 1957. Much to our surprise we were invited to join one of the two cricket teams formed by the monks one summer Sunday. Even more surprising was a sort of cricket field laid out on the most level, but still sloping, field near the Castel. However, it did have a marked and rolled gravel pitch with a roughly and erratically marked boundary, as well. We were given a cell to change into cricket togs, which took a little time. We were surprised that all the monks were waiting for us, fully togged and ready to go. We discovered that they all had their cricket gear on and only had to hoist their cassocks to be ready to play.

There were few spectators: only the British Ambassador with a few friends in tow and a perfectly equipped picnic basket resting on a shelf that folded out of the Rolls. At the other end of the social spectrum was an Italian and his son, sitting sideways on a donkey. His expression spoke volumes, watching Englishmen going out in the midday sun.

The view from the playing field, perched high in the landscape, had magnificent views of the surrounding countryside. This often resulted in not abiding by the cardinal (no pun intended) rule of keeping one's eye on the ball. It also explained the monks' abstemiousness at lunch, listening to the choir chanting in the loft. In clear contrast at the post-game drinks, unlike at lunch, wine was everywhere in evidence. No wonder we lost.

Of course, Rome is a particularly interesting city for an architect. Bernini's design of the piazza in front of St. Peter's made an impression on me. The piazza is dished, sloping down from the enclosing colonnade to the fountain at the centre. When crowded, each person can see the whole assembly, conveying a sense of the Catholic universe. With a flat surface each person sees only those immediately around him or her.

Nolli's 1748 map of Rome delineates the city's public space, the streets and squares, as well as interiors of churches and other public buildings. It shows a public realm that is at times intimate and other times grand, open and enclosed, linked and intermittent. Rome remains a profoundly satisfying city. I wonder if our cities will be as satisfying centuries from now.

• • •

Oxford was the setting for the greatest stroke of good fortune in a fortunate life — meeting my future wife. Lectures and seminars weren't compulsory, which meant I didn't attend many. However, at an economics seminar I was immediately attracted to one of the other students. She was intelligent and beautiful, but there wasn't a chance to introduce myself. A few days later I passed her on the High Street. I asked if she had been at a recent social event. She simply said "no" and walked on.

I used the new Bodleian library, which had the bibliography for most of the essays I was writing. Part of the motivation for those visits was an expectation that I might find Gillian there.

I did, but an offer to take her for coffee was turned down. I discovered that she had the same philosophy tutor — Philipa Foot — as I did. Those sessions were held in the tutor's home in North Oxford. As Gillian's session was ahead of mine, I assumed the winter coat draped over the stair balustrade was hers. I wrote a note, and dropped it into the coat pocket. A week went by with no response. This wasn't surprising, as I subsequently discovered that it wasn't her coat.

A second coffee invitation was also politely, but firmly, rejected. I thought that if a third invitation were turned down, that should be it. But the gods smiled that day, and she accepted. However, I had to borrow money from Tuppy Owen-Smith to pay for the coffee.

We began to see more of each other: dinner at the Boar's Head in Woodstock, picnicking with her friends on the grounds of Blenheim Palace, walks along the Isis and the university gardens, and attending my college Gaudy — a grand ball that ends at breakfast!

As I already had a degree (Bachelor of Architecture), I was permitted to complete the Oxford degree in two years. Gillian, however, took her degree in the standard three-year course (if intelligence was the criterion it should have been the other way around). For her last year I returned to South Africa, and we corresponded by airmail. While a formal proposal for marriage was never made, it was implicitly understood that we would marry. When it became clear to my parents that I was going to marry Gillian, there was strenuous objection, as Gillian wasn't Jewish. More for family peace and acceptance than religious convictions, it was decided that Gillian would convert to Judaism. Fortunately, Professor Dauber, one of the dons at All Souls College, became her tutor. A highly respected academic, he taught Gillian the best principles of Judaism.

It was arranged that we would marry in the Reform Synagogue in St. John's Wood (the Lords house opposite the Lord's cricket ground). Notwithstanding Gillian's conversion, my father refused to attend the wedding. My mother made every effort to do so, but her flight from South Africa was delayed in Athens, so she missed the ceremony, as well. My father's brother, Louis Diamond, and his wife, Annie, were in London at the time and acted *in loco parentis*, and Bill Ritchie, my friend from the architectural school in Cape Town, who was living in London at the time, was best man.

I borrowed my future father-in-law's car to pick up Louis and Annie at their hotel in Mayfair. I parked outside on the street and went in to fetch them. Louis was having difficulty with his cravat, which I helped him tie. This created a bit of a delay, and on exiting the hotel I found the car was gone. I explained to a bobby who was walking by in his measured gait, that my car had been stolen, that it was my wedding day, and that the ceremony was in half an hour. He asked where I had parked the car. I showed him and he explained that it probably hadn't been stolen. It had been parked in a no-standing zone, and was probably towed away. The bobby went to a police phone box and confirmed the car was in the police compound. In a short time a police car arrived, bell ringing, and took me to the police station. A burly sergeant, a Giles cartoon character, sitting behind a desk with arms folded, greeted me with, "I understand it's your wedding day."

"Yes, yes, I need the car to get to the wedding ceremony on time!" I replied in obvious distress.

"I'll tell you what, I'll lock you up overnight, and you'll thank me in the morning."

He was joking. I got the car, and we arrived at the synagogue on time (almost).

The next day, Gillian and I took the Orient Express train to Venice, where we began our married life. We boarded a ship in Venice bound for South Africa, via the Suez Canal and the east coast of Africa.

. . .

Gillian and I had assumed we would live our life in Durban. However, the African population was understandably growing increasingly restive, chafing against apartheid and the increasingly restrictive laws for people of colour. The government response was brutal. At a peaceful demonstration in Sharpeville, about seventy kilometres from Johannesburg, on March 21, 1960, police fired on the crowd, killing 69 people and wounding 180. Among the casualties were twenty-nine children. Many were shot in the back as they were peacefully dispersing. It was a turning point in the fight against authoritarian rule, and a chilling expression of rabid racism.

We had returned to a country that was increasingly divided and violent. From my office in Trust Towers, I watched the revolution in action. A large group of Black people approached city hall, intent on releasing political prisoners from jail. One of the few white people in the march was Anthony de Crespigny, a friend. He seemed to be deliberately courting arrest, and was disappointed when he wasn't.

A more violent revolution was being developed by a group called the Rivonia Five, led by Nelson Mandela. Hitherto, he had advocated passive resistance, but this had given way to acts of sabotage, such as blowing up power lines. Among the group was Arthur Goldreich, who had learned to make bombs as a member of the underground resisting British rule in Palestine. Goldreich was trained as an architect, and he'd designed the sets and costumes for a political musical titled *King Kong*. When the play ran in Durban, Arthur, an interesting man and a superb raconteur, stayed with Gillian and me.

Arthur was finally arrested and put into the notorious Marshall Street jail in Johannesburg. A guard was bribed to unlock his cell. Rope was provided for his escape. Once on the high prison wall, Arthur sensed that something wasn't right. A common means of dealing with prisoners was to shoot them when they tried to escape. He broke back into the jail. He did escape the next night, though.

He dressed as a Catholic priest and lodged in a monastery. Even the priests were unaware of his true identity. For a week the South African government searched for him. He was able to get a small plane to fly to Bechuanaland, now Botswana, a British protectorate where South Africa had no jurisdiction. He had the pilot pull right up to the door of the small airport so he could run inside and claim refugee status. The South African police blew up the plane, despite the fact that it was on British soil. Arthur eventually made his way back to Israel, and took a position teaching architecture at Bezalel Academy in Jerusalem.

Nelson Mandela and the other members of the Rivonia Five were not so lucky. They were arrested, stood trial, were convicted of treason, and were sentenced to life imprisonment.

I had considered a political career; it had been part of the impetus to go to Oxford. I could have accepted a safe parliamentary seat representing the United Party — the only party likely to oppose the National Party — but its liberal and

anti-apartheid policies were weak. And the Nats were strongly
entrenched, using police to brutally put down any sign of opposition. After the Rivonia trial, when Mandela and other African
National Congress leaders were given life sentences, I realized it
would take at least a generation to shake off the country's racist
shackles and have a democratically elected parliament.

Mandela served his sentence on Robben Island, off the coast
of Cape Town. When he arrived at the island dock, the Afrikaner
jailer, wielding a *sjambok* (a rhino-skin whip that could almost
cut someone in half), commanded, "*Loop, Kaffir, loop*" (Run,
nigger, run). Mandela replied that there was nothing in prison
regulations that required him to run. He said he would walk.
It is difficult to convey the courage that it took to take such a
position — out of sight and sound of any protection whatsoever.

Gillian and I didn't want to live in a fascist state, and we
thought if there were to be a revolution, as whites we would be
on the wrong side. At the time, we were making every effort to
bridge the colour divide, but we didn't want to bring up children in South Africa. I also came to recognize that any talent I
had was in architecture rather than politics.

After Sharpeville, Gillian and I imagined a violent future
in South Africa. It was natural to consider moving to the U.K,
given Gillian's English background and my familiarity with the
country. But we weren't enamoured of the rigid class system.
The vast potential of North America won out. I applied to the
University of Pennsylvania to take a Master's degree in architecture. The School of Architecture at UCT had developed
links with the University of Pennsylvania's School of Fine Arts
(which consisted largely of the School of Architecture) by virtue
of the outstanding UCT graduates who preceded me. While
the South African quota for admission to the United States was

oversubscribed, the one from the U.K. was not, and we were able to apply under Gillian's British passport. South Africa had imposed strict currency regulations, prohibiting the export of capital: we were to land in the U.S. with $400.

. . .

I have returned to South Africa from time to time, to visit and to lecture. The School of Architecture at the University of the Orange Free State (now called the University of the Free State) initiated an annual lecture named the Sophia Gray Lecture and I was invited to make the annual talk in 1999. The purpose of the lecture was to stimulate architectural discourse and to memorialize the first professionally active architect in Bloemfontein, and South Africa's first female architect, Sophia Gray. She was the wife of the Anglican Bishop of Cape Town, arriving in 1848. During her twenty-five year career Gray designed and built fifty-eight churches.

Along with the lecture there was an exhibition of each speaker's work. My fellow member of the UCT Student Representative Council, Albi Sachs, was invited to open my exhibition. During apartheid, Albi had been jailed and placed in solitary confinement. On release, he escaped to Mozambique, where a South African agent car-bombed him. He lost an arm and eye, but survived. He was rewarded by Nelson Mandela with a post on the Constitutional Court in post-apartheid South Africa.

After I made some remarks, Albi formally introduced the exhibition. "After listening to Jack," he said, "I tore up my speech to tell you that Jack has not lost the idealism and principles he had as a student." He could not have said anything better.

Bloemfontein had been an apartheid government stronghold, and its architecture was built during the Nats regime. As is always the case, the architecture was an inescapable expression of the culture. Its buildings most closely resembled those of Nazi Germany.

I was put up at a comfortable B&B just outside Bloemfontein. There were still security concerns, and doors were locked after 11:00 p.m. One night I returned from a reception later than that. I knew the front door would be locked, but didn't know the back door was, as well. I tried to open it, which set off an alarm. A man appeared, both hands clutching a revolver pointed at me. He was clearly very stressed. I explained that I was staying in the house. The incident indicated how much the white population was, and still is, living on edge. Insurance companies insist on razor wire on top of masonry walls to enclose single-family houses.

Helen Smit was another UCT classmate. Her father was murdered on his farm not far from Bloemfontein, the judicial capital of South Africa. He was a Supreme Court Justice. Two Black intruders demanded he hand over any firearms he had. He refused and was shot, but not fatally. He shot one of the intruders, and the second then murdered him. Such occurrences were not uncommon. White farmers, mostly Afrikaners, owned, and still own, a vast preponderance of the country's arable land, even in post-apartheid South Africa. The issue of land ownership reform has simply not been addressed. One result is the high incidence of attacks on farmers.

Besides the disastrously high unemployment rate and lack of education, the lack of affordable housing for the Black population remains one of the country's greatest deficiencies. Without constructing schools, clinics, and libraries along with housing, the new South Africa only repeats a version of the shantytowns from decades earlier. The government has done little to absorb vast numbers into the economy. The corruption is especially galling, coming in the wake of the selfless Mandela.

. . .

Years later, when David Peterson, leader of the Ontario provincial Liberal Party, became the new premier of the province, he sought people with his politics to help run the many public bodies the government controlled. The list filled a thick book.

I was asked which might interest me. It was assumed that I would opt for areas related to my architectural experience, such as planning boards, or bodies concerned with land use and development densities. Little was known of my life in South Africa, or of my efforts, however small, in opposition to apartheid, or of the anti-Semitism I experienced as a child. These have driven my passion for social justice. In consequence, rather than be involved in government bodies related to architecture, my preference was to act as Human Rights Commissioner, a role I held for five years.

Five

A New World

IN THE SUMMER OF 1961 WE ARRIVED IN PHILADELPHIA, a city that was hotter and more humid than Durban. That first night we stayed at a Holiday Inn near the university. It cost us $40, a tenth of our savings. We would need cheaper accommodation as soon as possible. After scouring the areas in Philadelphia with reasonable access to the university, we settled on an attic apartment in the city centre. With no insulation, the apartment was unbearably hot in high summer, and Gillian and I took turns lying in a cold bath to cool off.

To save money, I walked to classes in the morning, walked home in the evening, walked back after dinner, and back to the apartment at night to save the twenty-five-cent car fares.

Gillian was at first employed by the psychology department at the university, batting dogs with a rolled-up newspaper to gauge their reaction (not happy). She then applied to an employment agency for a position that would use her formidable intellect and mathematical mind. The employment agency inquired about her education, and she said she had a degree from Oxford. The employment officer asked where that was, and she told him it was in England. "Oh, that's why I've never heard of it," the officer said. Gillian was subsequently taken on by the Pen-Jersey transportation study, and in 1961 became one of the first to use a computer to analyze data. The computer filled a whole room.

· · ·

The University of Pennsylvania had a stellar architecture faculty. Along with Louis Kahn, there was Le Ricolais, an extraordinary French engineer; Aldo Giurgola, an erudite Italian architect of great talent; Ian McHarg, the revolutionary landscape architect; Robert Venturi, of contemporary mannerist fame; and an exceptional dean, Holmes Perkins, who had assembled this academic pantheon.

Louis Kahn's class was endlessly interesting. As a three-year-old Kahn had been badly burned and still carried the scars on his face. He couldn't have been taller than five-and-a-half feet. A visionary architect and brilliant draftsman, he was a graduate of the University of Pennsylvania, a Beaux Arts school at that time. His Richards Medical Building was being built on campus while I was there.

It is an important building in the history of architecture. One reason for this is that it resolved two antipodal factors. Kahn characterized the two as "served" and "servant" spaces.

The former — the laboratories — are glass enclosed. The latter — storage and other utility functions — are contained in concrete silos.

The composer Stockhausen, who gave a memorable lecture at Penn, described the resolution of polar opposites in any of the arts as the highest of artistic achievements. He generalized the polarities as the "individual" and the "dividual" (a word he invented): that is, pattern and object, or painterly and linear. An example in music is the power and sweep of Beethoven, compared to the minimalism of Philip Glass. In painting, Jackson Pollock's abstract and undifferentiated patterns versus Lucien Freud's portraits. Vermeer's work is notable for its resolution — a Vermeer can be viewed as a nonrepresentational composition or as a powerful genre depiction of domestic life.

In architecture, the polar opposites are in the spaces. In classical architecture the spaces are well defined: the enclosure of space has opacity, thresholds, corners, and finite fenestration. Its opposite is best illustrated by Mies van der Rohe's Barcelona pavilion at the 1929 International Exhibition. This encapsulated the essence of the modern movement — spaces flow into one another with no sense of a boundary between one space or another, the roof does not necessarily correspond to the space it covers, the partitions do not define spaces and are transparent. The polarities of contemporary architecture are those of well-defined volumes and the interpenetration of space in transparent structures.

Thus, contemporary architecture has a wide pallet of elements on which to draw for appropriate application, depending on function. Kahn's Richards building was a brilliant example of this resolution. Both it and his modest bathhouse near Trenton, New Jersey, were structures of epochal significance.

During one class, we had a visit from the equivalent classes at Yale and Harvard, whose students included Richard Rogers and Norman Foster. For the Yale visit Kahn asked for a piano — Lou was also an accomplished pianist. He put on a performance: talking; drawing on a blackboard with both hands at once to achieve a very large, symmetrical classical detail; and playing snatches of Bach on the piano. We met with Khan once a week, at which time he would use our work to expound on his approach to architecture, which was to get to its very essence. It was almost like Michaelangelo, or like Inuit carvers, who chisel stone to release what is inherently within.

Robert Lericolais's course was very popular, and was oversubscribed. To cut the numbers down, he devised a test for admission. A human skeleton hung from a scale at the front of the classroom. All he said was, "Tell me what you see."

A clue was the fact that the skeleton was hanging from a scale, which showed a weight of about twenty-five pounds. Thus the structure was one that could support a weight of at least 150 pounds, and often much more, that is, at least six times its weight: a very efficient structure-to-weight-bearing ratio. The structure was varied in its configuration, each component shaped for a separate function: the rib cage to protect vital organs; the limbs supported by relatively thin shafts, thickened at ends to spread loads and perform hinge movement; and a hollow flexible spine as a conduit for nerves. These particular responses to function were accomplished with the minimum of material.

The bones were strung together with wire clips, indicating the structure was good in compression, but poor in tension. In contrast, the structure-to-weight-borne ratio of most buildings is unnecessarily high and wasteful. In a world of diminishing resources, the need to design with an economy of means has become of overriding importance. Lericolais's lessons have never been more necessary.

On graduation, I applied to the University of California, Berkeley for a teaching position. The climate of California was much like that of the Cape in South Africa, far more salubrious than the boiling summer and freezing winters of Pennsylvania. I didn't hear from Berkeley and asked the dean what I should do. He surprised me by offering me a place as a studio master at Penn.

Being a studio master meant only three afternoons attendance a week, so I also accepted a position with Vincent Kling, a large, corporate office of reputable, if not brilliant, design reputation. I also took a position teaching night school at the Drexel Institute of Technology.

With this income, we first rented what was known as a "holy ghost" house in Society Hill, a fast-gentrifying inner-city area. The holy ghost term came from the narrow townhouse configuration, with one room for each of the three floors of the building.

For the Christmas holiday, we received an invitation from our friend Bill Bernhard to join him and his family in Palm Beach, Florida, where his grandmother had a house. As we now had a car — a used Renault — we accepted. However, on our drive down the car began to consume oil at an alarming rate. In Jacksonville we took the car to a garage. The garage owner told us that the odometer had been rolled back — the car had been driven for many more miles than that shown, and the engine needed replacing.

Back in Philadelphia, I went to the seller of the car, and claimed payment for the new engine, caused by their illegal tampering with the odometer. They essentially said, "get lost."

I went to the dean of law at the university, and asked for advice. He called the venerable law firm Dechert Price & Rhoads, who served notice on the second-hand car dealer — pay up, or see us in court. They paid up.

We bought a new car — a Volkswagon Beetle, and an air conditioner for our bedroom, which made Gillian happy; she was pregnant at the time. When she was due I dropped her off at the hospital and went to work. A few hours later I got a call: I had a son. Both Gillian and my parents were in Philadelphia at the time and my father held Andrew for the bris.

My teaching arrangement was ideal — a half post that allowed me to combine theory and practice. However, Vincent Kling's corporate firm wasn't appealing and I moved to Louis Kahn's office, where I quickly found that it was far better to be Kahn's student than his employee. The contrast between Kling's mercantilism and Kahn's poetic sensibility was vast. Kling understood pragmatism and profit in a difficult industry, while Kahn contemplated the noblest of architectural aims — to make a better world.

These are particularly Jewish characteristics — the material and the spiritual. When in dynamic balance, the accomplishments can be of great humanistic value. When one or the other is predominant, the result is crass materialism or empty ritual. (The exception, hopefully to prove the rule, would be Einstein.)

In Kling's office, the management of projects, especially the fees, was rigorous. Project managers filled out weekly balance sheets. Projects that were over budget were literally in the red — filled out on pink forms. Design reviews were conducted by Vincent with two yes men in attendance. To be one of those, a command performance, was known as being Kling for the day. When Vincent disagreed with the approach I took on a design, he said, "You have a fire in your belly." I wasn't sure it was a compliment.

Kahn's office lacked Kling's organization, to put it mildly. He died half a million dollars in debt. There were loyal members of the firm who tried to instill order, but without Lou's cooperation they were doomed to failure. He once threw a box of pastels at the putative manager. When Kahn got tired he would climb onto his drawing board and take a nap. His demeanour in the office was far more severe than in the studio at Penn. In the studio he would always try to find something positive in a student's work, but in the office his criticism could be harsh.

While in Lou's office I was assigned the design of a hospital in Dacca, Pakistan, to be a component of the National Capital Building complex. Lou was due for a visit to the site, departing on a Monday. I worked through Saturday, Saturday night, and Sunday. On Sunday evening I went home for a shower and a few hours sleep. When I returned on Monday morning Lou asked where I had been the previous night. He said, "You disappeared just when I needed you."

Jackie Kennedy visited when she was in the process of selecting an architect for the Kennedy library and Kahn made an effort to clean up the office for her arrival. I'm sure Lou charmed her, but his esoteric, even poetic, use of language might not have had the desired effect. His private speech went against the essential point of communication — to convey common meaning with clarity. My education in Wittgenstein at Oxford had emphasized such clarity. Ms. Kennedy may not have known what Lou was talking about. In the end, the commission went to I.M. Pei.

. . .

While I was teaching at Penn, Dean Holmes arranged for me to attend a conference for young architecture professors at the Cranbrook Academy, outside Detroit. One of those attending was an Australian, John Andrews, who taught architecture at the University of Toronto. We got on well, and he invited me to participate in reviews of student work. After several of these, John persuaded the chair of the department to offer me a job at the school. I was offered a post in the undergraduate program, which I turned down, as I did not want to provide training, but education. The University of Toronto did not have a post-graduate program, so it was agreed that I should set one up and run it. So Gillian and I emigrated once more, this time to Canada, and settled in Toronto.

During this time I was also offered the chairmanship of the school of architecture at the University of California, Berkeley. Gillian and I gave this serious consideration. However, as attractive as this offer was, the reasons not to accept were greater: despite assurances to the contrary, it would be difficult to develop a practice. More important we did not want to live in the USA — the Canadian political, social, and cultural systems, those with which we were familiar, suited us very well. To the great surprise of the selection committee I turned the offer down.

When we arrived in Toronto in 1963, I thought I had made a great mistake. It seemed a city of Presbyterian narrowness and architectural mediocrity. It took some time to realize there was more to Toronto than met the eye. A city of profound satisfaction slowly revealed itself, where the collective urban form is as important as the individual building, where continuous streetscapes are animated and safe, where there is a congenial mix of uses, and a nuanced but regular street grid.

The only buildings that broke the uniform street grid were public buildings, given pride of place that no private structure was accorded. They broke the rigid grid, dominating the vista. A natural ravine system also stood in contrast to the grid, meandering green lungs that provided relief to the man-made environment. It represented the best of the Canadian ethos — where the individual and the community are given equal importance, and public and private interests are in balance. Toronto was also on the cusp of its transformation from a provincial city to one of global significance.

Our first nights in Toronto were in the Four Seasons hotel on Jarvis Street. More motel than hotel, it had little to suggest the Four Seasons five-star hotels to come. A notice at the Faculty Club advertised a one-year house lease from a professor who was on sabbatical leave. It overlooked one of Toronto's ravines. Donald Coxeter, a mathematics professor with a focus on topology, a gentle soul (in contrast to his Dutch wife), who became as famous as a geometer can, agreed to lease the house to us.

In December 1963, Gillian and I were in New York, visiting Gillian's parents for Christmas. Her father Ken was Britain's trade commissioner to the U.S. Gillian was pregnant, due to give birth in late January 1964. But on December 22, Gillian complained of backache. The pain was coming in waves. We phoned the obstetrician in Philadelphia who had delivered our son Andrew. He said that if you can't make it to Philadelphia, head for Jersey City. I had visions of being stuck in a traffic jam in the Holland Tunnel, and having to be the midwife. We then called Arthur Helfet, a doctor friend from Cape Town who was spending his sabbatical at Mount Sinai hospital in New

York. He was an orthopaedic surgeon, not an obstetrician, but he called Columbia University then called us back to say the Woman's Hospital was expecting us.

It's a good thing they were. Twelve minutes after being admitted, Gillian gave birth to a beautiful, if premature, daughter. She was just above the five pound minimum, so avoided the incubator.

We returned to Toronto on a freezing winter day and there was no one at the immigration counter to register Alison Suzanne Katherine Diamond. I wasn't about to wait around for an official to appear, so we walked through customs and took a cab home. We later got an embarrassed call from the department of Citizenship and Immigration, asking if they could come and complete the formalities. During the visit the official asked me if we had any allergies or illnesses. I said yes: an uncommon dislike of waiting around cold reception areas with a newborn.

. . .

The lease on our house ended and we began the search for a permanent home. We had saved $10,000 of the $16,000 I had earned in Philadelphia by virtue of my three jobs. It was enough for a down payment on a house.

We found a three-storey house in Moore Park. The asking price was $32,000. I offered $30,000, with the expectation that it would saw off at $31,000. The seller insisted on $31,500. At that stage it was not a question of price, but of pride. However, Gillian asked if I wanted to lose the house over $500. I paid up.

On the east of the ravine, it was one of two original houses built in 1892, and had been converted to a rooming house during the Second World War. It needed extensive renovation.

Rabbi Avraham (Aba) Werner (b. Chaima).

Simma Gittle Werner (née Liebel).

Rabbi Werner (seated, right), at Zionist Congress, Basle, 1898.

Rabbi Werner's funeral, London, 1912.

Joseph Dimant.

Sarah Risa Dimant (née Gor).

(left to right) Louis Dimant, Joseph Dimant, and Jacob Diamond (born Dimant).

Jacob Dimant, top right; Sarah Risa and Joseph Dimant, seated, second and third from left.

Jacob Werner.

Rebecca Werner (née Abrams-Levy).

Bernard and Herman (standing, left to right), Ettie (centre), Rebecca and Jacob (seated), and Rachel (seated on floor) Werner.

Rachel and Jacob Diamond, January 1932.

Abel Joseph (Jack) Diamond, 1955. Born November 8, 1932.

Oxford vs. Australia, Diamond cross-kicking.

Diamond, Oxford Blues, scored winning tries against Australian Wallabies.

DIAMOND IS A GEM

**PIC
SPORT
PAGE
SIX**

STOP!

Logan
proves
actions
speak
louder
than
words

Oxford U. 12 pts., Australians 6

WALLABIES' scoring machine was blunted, taken apart and thrown on the scrap heap by fifteen dark blue shirted heroes of Oxford University.

They cared not for reputations, and refused to sit back and wait for the dazzling attacking moves which we all know the Aussies have stored up.

The Oxford men set out to dominate things from the first move. And, they did just that.

Led by England International Peter Robbins, an inspiration and a tremendous source of energy, the Oxford pack stormed into the game at top pressure.

Toast of Oxford was South African Jack Diamond who scored both the University tries. He normally turns out for the reserve XV, but was brought in on the wing because John Booth was unfit.

His first try polished off a brilliant piece of open Rugby in which Steve Wilcock, Brian Weston, Peter Sibley and Malcolm Phillips all handled.

But his later effort, using a piston-like hand-off to clinch the win when Oxford were three points up was a gem.

After Rob Wilson had kicked a forty-yard penalty for Oxford, Ron Harvey levelled matters, also from a penalty. It was in the immediate pre-interval spell that Oxford, for the only time looked in trouble.

MISJUDGED

More trouble came just after half-time when Wilson misjudged a rolling kick and White got the touch down.

Then came the best back movement of the game resulting in Diamond's first try, another penalty by Wilson and Diamond's final death blow to the tourists' hopes.

Mr. T. H. McClenaughan the Australian manager commenting on his team's defeat said: "It was not really a surprise. We took something of a risk in putting twelve new players in the side.

Diamond clinching the win for Oxford University.

First project, Albert Park, Durban, South Africa. Barrel vaults under construction, 2.5″ at peak, 7″ valley. Structural strength inherent in the form.

Gillian and Jack post wedding, St. John's Wood, London, Reform
Synagogue. August 11, 1959.

(left to right) Jacob, Abel (Jack), and Andrew Diamond. Chestnut Hill,
Philadelphia.

Gillian Mary Diamond (née Huggins). Born February 10, 1937.

Jack Diamond, mace bearer, and Teddy Kollek, mayor of Jerusalem, when Mayor Kollek received an honourary degree from the University of Toronto.

(left to right) Shimon Peres, Israeli foreign minister; John Manley, Canadian foreign minister; and Jack Diamond, architect, at the opening ceremony, Ministry of Foreign Affairs, Jerusalem.

(left to right) Valery Gergiev, conductor of the Mariinsky orchestra; Vladimir Putin, Russian president; and Jack Diamond. Opening celebration of the Mariinsky II, Saint Petersburg, Russia.

Family. (left to right) Tyler Whisnand, Jack and Andrew Diamond (standing); Linda Kitchen, Gillian Diamond, Suki Whisnand Diamond (seated); Hayden Whisnand, Daniel Diamond, Cole Whisnand, and Joshua Diamond (seated on floor). Sweet Pond, Lunenburg, Nova Scotia.

My mother visited us from South Africa, and I went to the airport to meet her. While I was gone Gillian put soiled children's nappies in the washing machine. Unfortunately, the plumbing contractor hadn't connected the washing machine to the drain. The flooded floor, next to the kitchen, wasn't the best way to introduce my mother to our new home.

This first renovation was done with a very small budget, and compromises — which I abhor — had to be made. Our second renovation was more ambitious and included replacing the crude entrance platform that stood in for the demolished porch with a porch consistent with late-nineteenth-century details. We built a swimming pool, and added a greenhouse that opened off the kitchen. But, it was only with the third renovation that we finally got it right. The living room was extended into the space the original porch had occupied. Below the living room we created a garage for two cars, and on the roof, a deck with an outdoor shower. All three fireplaces and their handsome mantles were restored. Gillian developed the garden with appropriate urbanity. Our children grew up in that wonderful family house. We lived there for forty-nine years.

• • •

When I was teaching we enjoyed the long university summer vacations, and we spent a number of them with Oxford friends, Teddy Millington-Drake and John Stefanidis, who had a house on the Greek island of Patmos. We travelled on cheap, extremely uncomfortable charter flights to Europe. I measured the distance between the seat and the chair ahead to be seven inches.

We took the ferry from Piraeus to Patmos, an overnight trip. First class meant sitting in the dining saloon, while third class was among the goats brought by Greeks returning to their islands. There was, at the time, no dock in Patmos to berth the ferry. A rectangular basket attached to a boom conveyed passengers to a small barge, then to shore.

Teddy's house was in Hora, an idyllic village that surrounds the hill-top monastery in which St. John wrote his *Divine Revelations*. Thick, whitewashed walls enclosed a courtyard shaded by lime trees. The courtyard floor was covered in Persian rugs, as there is dependably no rain during the summer. This was in the late sixties and early seventies, and there was only one telephone in Hora. The only sound at night was the tinkling of bells tied around donkeys' necks as they were driven out to graze in the early morning.

Our children wandered the village in complete safety. They would return with presents, though we had to make Andrew return the rabbits he was given. We were so enamoured of life on Patmos that we bought a ruin of our own. We decided to renovate it and make a holiday home. This despite the military coup in 1967, where a group of colonels took over the Greek government. Their seven-year regime changed life on Patmos. A dock was constructed to allow cruise ships to berth, and the town square was soon crowded with stalls selling cheap souvenirs. The simple joys of Patmos were disappearing. Jackie Kennedy paid a visit, and the Aga Khan bought a property. We sold our nearly completed house, making a small profit. This was opportune, as I needed the money to start a practice.

. . .

As soon as I could I became a Canadian citizen. In addition to becoming a citizen of the best of the western democracies, I could now visit countries from which I had been banned with my South African passport. The first place I visited, however, was South Africa, to visit my mother, my sister Stella, her husband, Sidney, and their children. My own children hadn't met their cousins or aunt or uncle. We stayed in Durban with family, then flew to Nairobi, where we stayed at the Norfolk Hotel. It was owned by the Block-Hirschfelds, distant Israeli relatives on my mother's side. (In 1976, after the raid on Entebbe and the rescue of the Israeli hostages, the hotel was bombed — it had been discovered that Hirschfeld had organized the refuelling of the rescue aircraft.)

Hirschfeld was a member of the Haganah, the underground resistance movement during the British mandate. When the Balfour Declaration determined that Palestine should provide a home for Jews, it had a provision for Arab interests, as well. The British administration took these to the extreme by imposing limits to Jewish immigration. This despite the fact that most immigrants were Holocaust survivors. Refugees, on arrival in Israel, were sent back to Cypress, to be once more imprisoned in wire cages. However, the Haganah organized the illegal entry of Jews. A group was being held in pens near Jaffa, waiting deportation. Hirschfeld told us that he and his compatriots raided the pen and freed the refugees. But one of the captives began to scream. To silence her one of the Haganah put his hand over her mouth. Unfortunately, she suffocated and died. It was later discovered that she was neither Jewish nor a Holocaust survivor, but a German.

We had come to Nairobi to see the famous game reserves. We visited the Serengeti, Ngorongoro, and Masai Mara reserves in a van and a Land Rover jeep. We had the good fortune to arrive at a time of great migration. Thousands of tightly packed wildebeest moved across the landscape, giving the impression that the horizon was heaving.

We were charged by a rhinoceros, which may have seen the jeep as a threat. We were separated by a wide ditch, however, which deflected its charge. In lion country the jeep had a flat tire and our driver placed us at the four corners of both vehicles to keep a lookout while he changed the tire. We saw a leopard take down a deer and take it up a tree. Early one morning we came across a herd of elephants. A bull elephant began trumpeting and flapping its ears. We were on a narrow dirt road surrounded by dense bush. I said to the driver to get out of there quickly. He replied, "Slowly!" and reversed at a snail's pace.

· · ·

The sixties was a time of social upheaval in general and in architectural schools in particular. In Toronto, the form it took was to abjure all formal teaching, including the basics of structure, history, and other foundations of the profession. The view was that if an architect needed that information, he or she would find it somehow.

I continued to teach the lessons of history and to use critiques for design reviews. Did a design satisfy the student's internal objectives while addressing external consistency? One of the reviews was attended by what was called the Red Guard — students named for Mao's student revolution in China — who aggressively dismissed my approach. The department was divided and I finally received a letter — I was fired. As it obviously wasn't for justifiable cause, I took the matter to the academic council and was subsequently reinstated. Then I promptly quit.

The next day I was offered a place in the environmental studies program at York University. This required only three afternoons a week and I was able to pursue my dream of actually designing buildings.

John Andrews offered me a place in his growing practice, which I took. It came with the promise of a partnership, but he didn't honour that promise and so I resigned within a year. I saw no prospect of a practice of my own so I reluctantly accepted a job in a corporate firm as their chief designer. Before taking up the position, Gillian and I attended the company's Christmas party. I looked around at their clients and consultants and instantly decided it was not for me. Next morning, Gillian and I discussed the situation, with me in tears. I said I would rather sell socks at Eaton's, a large department store, than practice the kind of architecture I'd be doing at that firm.

In addition to part-time teaching, in 1966 I had taken on the job of editor at the professional journal *Architecture Canada*, which involved an annual trip across Canada, visiting our representatives in each major city. It allowed me to see current projects and also to more rapidly develop a sense of the country and its culture.

In Edmonton, the journal's representative was asked by a dean at the University of Alberta to recommend an architect to develop a master plan for the campus. At the time there was a rapid expansion of academic facilities across the country, and I had written critically of much that was being done. Perhaps the most trenchant example was that of Brock University, a new institution that was set in green fields instead of an urban context. Nearby St. Catharines was beginning to suffer from reduced industrial output. There would have been a double benefit from locating the university within the city — the economic benefits of the university would have helped to replace the lost industrial output, and the university wouldn't have needed to provide as much housing, food services, and book and other retail supply services.

I had critiqued other plans, but had yet to create my own. Our Edmonton representative told the dean that a local architect could do a satisfactory job with the University of Alberta campus, but if he wanted something better, he should hire me. The dean interviewed me, and, to my surprise, I was hired. It was a leap of faith, as I couldn't show him much that I'd built to demonstrate my approach to planning and design.

This led to a series of other Edmonton projects, among them the Student Union housing building, which was featured in *Time* magazine. This also led to being awarded the commission to design the Citadel Theatre in Edmonton. These seminal projects at the university and in the performing arts became the foundation of my future practice.

. . .

I had taught in the School of Architecture at the University of Toronto for almost six years (1964 to 1970). To make the academic program more relevant, I had given the students urban design and architectural projects based on actual conditions in the city. At that point, design projects at the school tended to be non-urban projects for the privileged. This at a time when the world was rapidly urbanizing. So I set design problems in the city, with real issues to be addressed, with all the opportunities and problems that they presented.

Unfamiliar with Toronto, I had approached the city planning department and asked what was the most difficult problem

they faced. A neighbourhood near the university that accommodated low-income residents in traditional semidetached and
attached two- and three-storey housing was under threat of
demolition. It was zoned to be the site of a large electrical sub-
station. Despite the low income, the community was remark-
ably stable. This stability was augmented by local food stores
and other essential retail commodities that were well suited to
their customers. Shopkeepers knew their customers well enough
to extend credit, something that was necessary for people who
had little access to banking or other credit systems.

Such residents, when displaced, don't always relocate to
similar downtown locations. They move back to the towns or
villages from which they came. So the community would have
been deprived of low-skilled labour. The community also had
a large component of Chinese immigrants. They were conveniently located close to Chinatown, its commercial heart on
nearby Spadina Avenue. Their removal would further affect
the subtle social and economic web on which the community
thrived.

The official plan demarcated the area as industrial. A careful assessment was made of the physical condition of the existing housing. The houses in the western sector of what became
known as the Hydro Block, an ironic name for the neighbourhood, were of sufficient scale and construction standard to be
converted into multiple dwelling units. However, the eastern
half of the block was in poor condition. Demolishing the eastern half would make it possible to build housing at a similar
scale to the western section, but at a higher density in order
to accommodate the urgent need for low-to-moderate income
housing in the inner city. The continuity of the streetscape
could be maintained, as well. The objective was to achieve

multiple housing that shared some of the characteristics of a single-family house — a street address and soundproofing between units. The design, a five-storey building, achieved a density of eighty units an acre. Three of the five first-floor apartments had independent access to the street. Throughout the design exercise the class was in close contact with the resident population, in order to discover its wants and needs. They were out in the real world, gaining an understanding of the specific needs of a neighbourhood.

At the same time a progressive city council came to power, along with progressive Mayor David Crombie. Among its reform measures was the establishment of a non-profit housing corporation. The local community made their councillor aware of the work we were doing at the university. As a consequence, the city became involved in the Hydro Block, first changing the zoning to eliminate the industrial category, then undertaking the actual implementation of the principles of our work in the master's class and the attention we had lavished on residents and location alike. At the residents' insistence, it was determined that I was to be the architect for the project.

The project was a success and it led to a similar project in the Regent Park neighbourhood. At the time, Regent Park, notwithstanding its high-rise form, was stigmatized as a ghetto, filled with immigrants who often had low-paying jobs and needed to be near the city core. It was seen as a high-crime neighbourhood and largely viewed as hopeless. Unlike the Hydro Block, the land to be redeveloped here was privately owned, and the developers resisted any modifications to their plan. Their idea was to demolish the existing housing and replace it with more high-rise towers that would have little or no relationship to the street. Given the recalcitrance of the developer, who in reality was not a contractor but merely an assembler of a prevalent construction system, (as the developers put it, we make socks, not shirts), the city took over the land to implement our design. This entailed renovating the street-related housing into apartment units, and constructing a mid-rise apartment structure on the lane at the rear the property.

Both Regent Park and the Hydro Block were unusual projects at the time. The CBS program *60 Minutes* got wind of them and produced a segment on the work we had done. The exposure from that show was a welcome turn of events for my now-growing practice.

. . .

In 1967, Canada's centennial year, I had been invited by the curator of the Art Gallery of Toronto (now the Art Gallery of Ontario), to design an exhibition about cities. I entitled it *This City Now*, and illustrated Toronto's strengths and potential future. This led to a commission to redesign a property in Yorkville, via the friendship between the head of the gallery, Bill Withrow, and Dick Wookey, a broker who had acquired the site. Yorkville has since become an expensive retail area in Toronto, but at the time it was a hive of coffee houses filled with hippies listening to Joni Mitchell and Neil Young and smoking pot.

The property was at the northeast corner of Avenue Road and Yorkville Avenue, a collection of two groups of semide-tached houses. This was when Le Corbusier's approach to city planning was in vogue. He advocated placing buildings in park-like settings. This was considered avant-garde, and influenced city planning almost everywhere. Had we demolished the old houses, any new structure would have to meet bylaw requirements and be set back from the street, per Le Corbusier, interrupting the continuous streetscape. Instead, we renovated the houses for new uses — shops and offices — and built more space around a courtyard in what had been the back yards of the houses. Not least among the urban benefits was more retail frontage than a setback arrangement would have yielded.

My fledgling firm occupied the attic floor of one of the buildings of York Square. Initially it was just myself, a receptionist who was also the bookkeeper, and two architectural assistants. It was at this point that I invited Barton Myers to come up from Philadelphia to join me. He had been at Penn, in the undergraduate program, graduating a year after I did. We got along well at Penn and I invited him to Toronto. The firm's name was later changed from Diamond Associates, Architects and Planners, to Diamond and Myers. The partnership didn't last, though. There was both a clash of egos and a difference in philosophy. Myers valued technology, and designed a steel house on stilts that was spectacularly unsuited to Toronto's climate. It was a triumph of aesthetic over purpose, and I was philosophically opposed to the idea.

By this time, I had articulated design principles that I was incorporating into my practice. Among them was the idea of technology as aesthetic. You need to design for the existing climate. In alpine locations, roofs are steep, some at forty-five degrees, to shed snow; in Mediterranean climates roof generally are effective at thirty degrees to shed winter rain; and in desert locations, with minimal rainfall, roofs are flat.

In hot, wet, tropical zones, the abundant timber provides for an open-frame structure to allow the free flow of air in a climate of minimal diurnal temperature change. The frame structure supports palm-frond thatching to shed tropical deluges. By elevating the floor of the building on stilts, insect and reptilian encroachment is minimized.

As the tropical structures maintain maximum openness, desert light is best served by minimal apertures. Windows are the irises of traditional architecture. Given the limits to building material in desert circumstances, buildings are made with thick walls made from sand. These warm up slowly during the day, and cool slowly at night, accommodating the wide diurnal temperature ranges. In northern European architecture, where the incidence of sunlight is low, such as in Holland or Scotland, windows are commensurately large.

An underrated architecture in its adaptation to context and available means of construction is the historic architecture of the Western Cape province in South Africa. Known as Cape Dutch architecture, it melded Dutch and French Huguenot cultures and the craftsmanship of Malay slaves. Thatch roofs were undergirded by a "brand solder," a fire-resistant clay brick layer above the board ceiling below. Masonry and plaster walls, particularly over entrance doors, provided an ember-free zone for the safe evacuation of precious furniture and other possessions. Plaster moulding gave emphasis to the entrance door below. Sliding-sash fanlights over the Dutch door afforded more interior natural illumination in inclement weather. A vine-covered pergola over the front stoep provided shade in summer, and, with the shedding of leaves, admitted more light in winter.

More familiar are the wood-framed, wood-clad houses of North America. Shingle, clapboard, and board-and-batten are not merely ways to enclose and waterproof a building, but are used as decorative elements that give scale, particularly domestic scale, to buildings of great charm.

. . .

Early in my practice, I had few connections and few examples of my work. I hadn't grown up in Toronto, did not have a social network, and did not belong to any clubs. Even after the success of York Square, it was difficult to win a commission. It was hard enough to find out what projects were in play. After failing in five consecutive attempts at winning commissions, I wasn't sure I could get up off the floor. But perseverance is a crucial ingredient of success.

After the Diamond Myers partnership broke up, my key commission was for a new YMCA building in downtown Toronto. In the midseventies, the YMCA was in the process of redefining itself. It no longer exclusively served a Christian constituency in multicultural Toronto, and had abandoned its residential function. It was concentrating on cultural and fitness activities, but it was in competition with the proliferating fitness clubs.

Over lunch, before our presentation to the selection committee, I brainstormed with Don Schmitt, who would eventually become my partner. Don had graduated from the University of Toronto, worked for a while in James Sterling's office in London, then joined my office as a junior.

Most fitness clubs had a fairly standard layout that separated various functions — gym, exercise space, etc. We presented design ideas that included an open stairway that traversed the height of the building. From each landing all the facilities and programs would be visible, the first step in gaining a member's interest. The members could see yoga and exercise classes, making them more accessible and less intimidating for those who wanted to join. We encouraged interaction among members with a flexible space where paths through the building crossed. This space, with very large sliding doors and seating that was retractable, could become a social hub of the building, a "town square." When closed up, with the raked seating fully deployed, it became a theatre.

The careful attention to the client's needs, and a design that addressed factors that they had considered, and some that they had not, won us the commission. Once it was built, members who joined for one program often joined others, because of the transparency of the design. The Toronto Y became the most successful Y in the world.

This approach served us well in subsequent commissions. We were determined not only to get a sense of what the client's needs were, but to gauge what was happening in their field. University buildings were undergoing a transition similar to that in the fitness world. The barriers between disciplines were breaking down and the occupants of buildings needed both interaction between fields of study and transparency.

When we entered the competition for the Life Sciences building at the University of British Columbia, we had never taken on a project of this size and function. I consulted with Dr. John Evans, who had gone through the process of building a medical school at McMaster University in Hamilton, Ontario, and subsequently became president of the University of Toronto. A man of great intellect and humanity, he met with me to discuss the field of life sciences. I asked him where that field was going. He said that in the twentieth century each professional field was self-contained and had rigid boundaries. For example, architects and engineers were in separate worlds, and, on campuses, in separate buildings, and this was true of the life sciences, as well. Research initiatives were closely guarded, and compartmentalized, and the existing architecture reflected that.

But those separate silos began to break down. There was a need for greater interdependence among disciplines. In the health sciences, for example, the dialysis mechanism for diabetic patients was invented by a petroleum engineer: it is simply a filtration system. Research into genome discoveries means that legal and ethical concerns need to be addressed. New and necessary interactions among physics, chemistry, biochemistry, and a host of other fields are required. Where once the disciplines were essentially separate entities, they now need to interact. This became the central principle of our design approach.

The UBC Life Sciences Centre, therefore, required the housing of medical training and research, anatomy, biochemistry, molecular biology, cell biology, medical genetics, and bioinformatics. I developed a series of design options for our interview at UBC that had three separate five-storey wings, connected by two atria. Not having any experience designing academic buildings became an advantage. My competitors talked only of what they had done. I talked of what could and should be done within a rapidly changing health-sciences field. We won the commission.

This success extended to other projects — the life sciences complex at Montreal's McGill University, the Li Ka Shing learning and research centre at St. Michael's Hospital, and the SickKids research tower, both in Toronto. (Don Schmitt was the principal in charge of this significant project.)

I realized early on that architecture sometimes evolves through the blind following of trends. What appears to be progress is really just inertia. It is necessary to challenge assumptions, to find forms and materials that express a building's purpose, and to create spaces that inspire awe, not from pyrotechnics, but from the elegance of their ideas. Universities are rooted in tradition, yet increasingly charged with the challenge of innovation. I recognized this tension and the changing nature of education and research, and the firm's designs reflect that.

In creating university buildings, the nature of education itself is sometimes overlooked. There are financial pressures to realize as much functional space as possible and to reduce the ratio between a building's square footage and its usable area. This can be a false economy. Formal knowledge is communicated in lecture halls, but new knowledge is often the result of casual interaction outside of the formal program. Architecture can foster that interaction.

As class sizes expand into the hundreds, the demands of lecture halls start to resemble the demands of concert halls. Sightlines and acoustics are critical. Performing arts facilities and university buildings became two of the pillars of our practice.

. . .

There are no architecture courses that I know of that teach one how to build a firm. I feel that establishing the firm is one of my best achievements, though it wasn't a smooth road.

I had established a set of architectural principles that were becoming the bedrock of my practice. Among them were to achieve the greatest utility, the easiest method of construction, and absolute simplicity. I embraced an economy of means, and rejected the imposition of random dramatic forms that ignored the needs of the space and client. This meant paying attention to both the context and the content of a building, the street and surrounding area, recognizing its social responsibilities. The aesthetic of the building should reflect its purpose, not the ego of the architect.

The firm continued to grow and, in 1970, we needed more space. A manufacturing building that once housed the Eclipse White Ware Company came up for sale on King Street West. Two sisters had inherited the building and wanted to sell. Manufacturing had long since fled the city's core and the market for the building was limited. It was a sturdy brick and beam structure that could, with some imagination and careful expenditure, house our offices as well as other retail and commercial enterprises.

It was difficult to convince clients that providing new life to old structures was viable. I thought if my office occupied part of the space, it might help convince them. I wasn't sure we could afford the building, so I approached Ed Mirvish, one of the few entrepreneurs at that time who was investing in real estate west of Avenue Road. (Friends would say to me "*West* of Avenue Road, Jack?" as if I were quite mad.) Mirvish was a colourful character who had made his fortune from an idiosyncratic department store that sold discount goods, and had then taken on a theatrical enterprise, buying the theatre building a block away. I asked if he was interested in becoming a financial partner in the venture. Ed thought it was an interesting proposition but he'd never had a partner in his life. He said, "You do it. If it doesn't work out, I'll take it on." He was as good as his word. He never attempted to *gezump* me, even though he recognized the potential of the project.

I persuaded a contractor to renovate one floor for ourselves, with a commitment to pay him over time. It was, in effect, a show home for prospective tenants, exhibiting the refinished wood floors, beams, columns, and ceilings, the cleaned exposed-brick walls, the new windows, and the exposed circular-duct air conditioning system.

Those who visited our renovated floor were impressed, but then they would inspect the unfinished floors and return crestfallen. They simply couldn't believe the unfinished space could be made to match our renovated floor. A lucky break came when the *Toronto Telegram* newspaper folded, and senior members started a new paper called the *Sun*. They had heard of our building, and inquired about space for their new enterprise. We arranged for them to temporarily occupy an unrenovated floor while we renovated space for them. The *Telegram* closed on a Friday, and the *Sun* rose on Monday.

Along with Don Schmitt, both Kevin Garland, a planner, and Paul Syme, an architect, became associates and the name changed to A.J. Diamond and Associates, Architects. We celebrated at a restaurant on Queen Street with a perogie lunch. The waitress was a Holocaust survivor, with numbers tattooed on her arm. Kevin eventually left to take an executive position at the Canadian Imperial Bank of Commerce, and Paul became an academic. Don continued to grow in capability and became an equal partner.

I took out a second mortgage to renovate the entire building. By virtue of the *Sun*'s profile, we soon had the building fully rented. The ground floor became La Cantinetta, an Italian restaurant, and Doug Creighton, the *Sun*'s editor-in-chief, had a table set aside for himself and his colleagues. Eventually Ed Mirvish did buy our building.

It had been a satisfying experience to repurpose a derelict manufacturing building, rather than see it either torn down to make way for something new or continue to live as a dusty warehouse.

Hugh Casson once remarked that New York is a place where they tear down permanent buildings to put up temporary ones,

Perhaps we no longer believe in stability or continuity. The lack of action to protect endangered species, or to prevent climate change, would seem to show that we don't care about the life of future generations or even about the preservation of our planet. In North America, by and large, we seem only to want to ensure that a building lasts its amortization period. What does this tell us about buildings that took two hundred years to build and are with us still?

When we moved into the King Street West offices the firm consisted of about twenty people. But it continued to grow until, once again, we needed more space. We moved to Berkeley Castle, a group of industrial buildings that we converted to mixed-use retail and office space. The five buildings had originally housed Toronto's first knitting mill. Built in 1868, they were on what was then the waterfront, before landfill extended Toronto's shoreline. When we began our renovation, the complex had actually been condemned. We demolished one of the buildings to create a courtyard, and Berkeley Castle would be our home for twenty years.

We occupied part of the building and rented the rest. By 1989, there were forty or so members in the firm. That year the recession decimated real estate values across the city. Berkeley Castle had been mostly rented at $16 a square foot. With the recession, we went from 90 percent occupancy to 40 percent — at $4.50 per square foot. And at that moment most of our architectural contracts were completed, with no new commissions coming in. The firm was in danger of going under.

To survive, we needed to cut costs. We went from forty people to fourteen; I had to let twenty-six people go, many of whom had partners and children. It was the most painful episode of my career. I had financial partners in the building — Herbert Leistner and Al Hertz. We went to our mortgage company and renegotiated the interest rate. We offered a choice of alternatives: reduce the rate, or take back the building. They had enough buildings in their possession and offered a rate we could afford on the promise that, when we were more profitable, we would revert to the previous rate.

Sadly, Herbert and his wife died in 2000 in a small plane that Herbert was piloting, crashing into Lake Huron in a dense fog. Seven years later, Al Hertz died of cancer. I inherited new partners, family of the deceased partners, an arrangement that didn't work out and only emphasized how important trust is: something I had enjoyed and honoured with my original partners. We left Berkeley Castle and Don Schmitt and I bought a building on Adelaide Street West, where we have remained.

The firm had grown from a single practitioner to one with employees, from being a doomed partnership to a company with associates who had a stake in the enterprise, to a partnership, and finally became an incorporated company (Diamond Schmitt Architects Inc., or DSAI) with twenty shareholders and three hundred employees. Something I learned during this evolution is that a change in magnitude requires a change in kind, but the overriding objective was to reap the benefits of a large firm while maintaining the character and spirit of a small studio. Against great odds, the firm has achieved a sense of family. That is a business cliché, but one that holds true.

My ideal had been the Virtuosi di Roma — a chamber music group, each member of which could have had a stellar solo career. As an ensemble, however, they were better than each of them alone. This is the principle on which I have based the organization and culture of the firm.

Six

The Much-Promised Land

SEEN FROM THE AIR, TEL AVIV LIES IN A NEAT FORM, THE buildings, until the end of the twentieth century, mostly of the same four- or five-storey height. It's as if the streets and parks were cut into the chalk-coloured clay, rather than placed on what was, until the 1920s, a desert.

I was in Israel because I'd received the commission to design the new city hall in Jerusalem. The cab driver who took me from the airport to Jerusalem spoke little English, but we made ourselves understood. The Hebrew spoken in Israel has a notably different accent from that of diaspora religious services, almost Arabic with its glottal stops and throaty consonants. This is the result of modern Hebrew being based in the Sephardic (Spanish) rather than the Ashkenazi (European) tradition.

The country was wonderfully green from winter rain, the groves of orange trees beautifully groomed. Soft grasses covered the stony plain. We began to climb the low limestone hills, approaching the Latrun intersection. Context is a critical element of architecture, and in Israel the context is complex and ancient. A tank, mounted on a block, is the monument to the capture of the Arab-held British police station by the fledgling Israel army in 1948 during the War of Independence. The police station commands the approach from the coastal plain to the foothills that lead to the Judean hills and Jerusalem.

After Latrun the hills get larger as the road climbs the narrow defile between the flanking heights. Scattered along the route are the metal frames of home-made "armoured" vehicles that ran the Arab gauntlet in 1948 to relieve the siege of Jerusalem. On each vehicle a date is stencilled on the rust-proof paint, the date on which the vehicle was destroyed, probably along with its young driver and precious cargo. They knew the chance of success was small, and I invariably have a frisson at their selfless bravery.

The cypress and cedar, now mixed with Jerusalem pine, became thicker and taller as the road climbed. Where glimpses of the land can be seen, it is layered in limestone, a geological *mille feuille*. To the west was a fine, arcaded mansion, a French seminary. There are tales of how the monks, pro-Arab at the time, allowed their buildings to be used by snipers. In 1948 it seemed inconceivable to some European powers that Jews could defeat Arab armies, especially the Arab legion, trained by the legendary Glubb Pasha.

We wound through the foothills, past the memorial forest. Six million trees have been planted — different species of cypress, pine, and poplar representing the men, women, and children murdered by the Nazis between 1938 and 1945. Six million is a number that has no impact in the abstract. But to see the huge forest, covering hill after hill, aroused the same desolate sadness I had when wandering the cemeteries on the Marne and the Somme. Innocent young people, with so much promise, so much to give the world, fellow human beings, slaughtered.

I was staying at the King David Hotel, which had been the headquarters of the British high command during the days of the British Mandate. An underground organization led by Menachem Begin, the future prime minister, blew up a wing of the hotel in July 1946, killing several senior British officers.

My room had a breathtaking view of the walls of the old city, built by Sulieman the Great in the sixteenth century and rebuilt during the Ottoman empire. The walls had once again been restored, and the landscaped Kidron and Hinon valleys set off the walls to advantage. The walls are important in tracing the four-thousand-year history of the city. They grew from the City of David, built near the spring of Shiloah, now the Arab village of Silwan. It was on the threshing floor, above the village on Mount Moriah, that the first communal rituals must have taken place. This site gained religious significance over time and subsequently became the site of the temple of Solomon and later the third of the holy places of Islam. We can be reasonably sure that this is where Abraham, Christ, and Muhammad prayed.

My great-grandfather's sister had been in the first *aliyah* from Finland in 1881. "Aliyah" in Hebrew is literally to go up, but colloquially means to migrate to Eretz Israel, the soil of Israel. Chai Malka Homer and her husband drained swampland and started planting vines. He died of malaria, and her manager robbed her of her savings. She sold the vineyard to the Rothschilds, who started the first wine cooperative in Palestine. I visited her grave on the Mount of Olives, a short distance from the garden of Gethsemane. The family had replaced the gravestone slab that had been vandalized during the Jordanian occupation from 1948 to 1967. I placed a small stone on the slab as is the custom, and felt a connection, but, strangely, not as strong as the connection I felt with the builders of Jerusalem's ancient walls.

· · ·

The city hall commission had come by a curious route. One of my former students — Ron Soskolne — had been hired by Olympia and York, the Reichmann family's real estate development company. In 1988, the Reichmanns were approached to provide their expertise in land development in Israel. Ron suggested to Albert Reichmann that I accompany him on a reconnaissance tour of the sites the Israelis had in mind.

The ones we saw were on the ocean between Tel Aviv and Jaffa, and those in Jaffa itself. We concluded that none of them were worth pursuing. During our visit, the city engineer of Jerusalem met us and suggested the Reichmanns finance a much-needed city hall, using their expertise to see that it was done in an effective, professional, and businesslike manner.

I subsequently received the commission to design the new city hall from Albert Reichmann. Zev Vered, an Israeli developer living in Ottawa, joined forces with the Reichmanns to take on the project. His youngest son, Ron, was appointed as liaison, and Zev's brother, who lived in Israel, was project overseer. After interviewing three Israeli architectural firms, we chose Kolker Kolker Epstein as our local partners for the project.

I conceived it more as a campus or precinct, deliberately designed not to have defined edges, but to integrate with it the surrounding city. This proved to be a challenge. When I received the commission, a zoning ordinance and a building design were in place that symbolically and physically turned the municipal centre's back on Arab Jerusalem, and would demolish all the historical buildings on the site. I appealed to the project managers on the grounds of efficiency, and to Mayor Teddy Kolleck on the grounds of municipal equity, to allow me to change the ordinance. Both supported the idea. I wanted a building that combined modern efficiency and historic sensitivity, and I wanted to restore existing buildings and create a civic plaza equally accessible from all points of the compass for both Arabs and Jews. Medieval maps show Jerusalem as the centre of the universe, uniting Asia, Africa, and Europe. Surely all its citizens, Muslim or Jew, Christian or Druze, should have common ground at city hall.

All other public spaces in Jerusalem are religious ones: the plaza next to the western wall of the temple of Solomon for the Jewish faith, the square next to the church of the Holy Sepulchre for Christians, and the platform on Haram al-Sharif for Muslims. The joke in Jerusalem was that if you wanted to hold a political protest, you had to go to Tel Aviv.

When we began removing the overburden off the rock base on the site, we came across archaeological relics — a small aqueduct, coins, and some oil jars from the First and Second Temple periods (980 and 450 BCE, respectively), one bearing the seal of Solomon's royal granary. These were taken off to the Israel Museum. I was concerned about the aqueduct that was cut into the rock base, thinking it would hold up construction. But eleventh-century (CE) artifacts aren't considered to be of great antiquity here, and the aqueduct was simply measured, drawn, and photographed, and construction proceeded. It wasn't just archaeologists surveying the site; rabbis, priests, and mullahs prowled. A friendly anthropologist was sure all the bones we discovered were animal bones.

One find did stop the work: a Herodian stone. This could have proved to be of great significance. The location of the third wall, built in the reign of Herod, if found, would finally determine the location of the crucifixion of Christ (Joshua ben Yosaif). The reason for this is that Josephus, the Jewish army commander of the Galilee who turned historian of the Judean-Roman wars, provides the measurement of the distance between the second and third walls. Christ, being a Jew, would have been either crucified or buried outside the walls of the city. Thus the discovery of the position of the third wall would fix the position of the second. And the stone seemed to be one that could have been used for such a wall.

More digging uncovered the foundations of a Crusader leper colony, which would have also been built outside the walls. It was concluded that the Herodian stone had been cannibalized by the Crusaders to build the leper colony. So this wasn't the location of the third wall. The subsurface work then began, blasting rock for an eight-hundred-car garage below the plaza and stabilizing eleven of the twelve existing buildings to be saved.

. . .

Whenever I could, I took my small pocket sketchbook and watercolours and walked around the old city sketching and painting. I never see anything really well until I draw it. It comes out right if I draw what is actually there, and not what my mind imagines is there. It is odd how perceptions affect the way one sees things, the minds' eye changing proportions from the way they actually are.

Walking around, I suppose I looked like a tourist, a North American, a Jew. This meant a hard indifference in any dealings with Arabs. As soon as I stopped to draw and paint, however, there was a change in attitude. There was discussion about Arab architecture first, and inquiries about where I came from next. The fact that I am Canadian also had a softening effect. I usually asked a local shopkeeper for a glass of water for painting, which gave him a claim over me and made further discussion easier, especially as I would thank him in Arabic, using one of the few Arabic words I have learned other than the terms for the various finishes for stonework (*tubzeh* — "roughly dressed"; *taltish* — "medium dressed"; *musamsam* — "finely dressed"; and *mutabeh* — "bush-hammered").

. . .

I designed the facades of the city hall to be clad in bands of rose and ochre limestone, a Mamluke device used by the splendid Arab architects of the sixteenth century to create a larger scale than the individual stone. This was achieved by having two courses of a reddish-brown stone alternate with two courses of stone in a pale ochre colour. The limestone, known as Jerusalem stone, actually comes from Galilee and the West Bank. Galilee wasn't a problem as it lies inside Israel's borders, but the rose-coloured stone comes from Arab quarries in the West Bank. The producer was threatened with death by Palestinians if he supplied us with the stone we needed. I feared we wouldn't get the contrast I wanted as the stone we did have was not markedly rose in colour. In the end, we were able to source the stone we needed and our supplier remained unharmed.

Jerusalem's complicated history and politics are reflected in the design. The north-south axis of the complex replicates the experience of the souk. This route is varied by light and shade, enclosure and openness, in contrasting small and large dimensions. It starts out in a narrow top-lit shopping arcade that is aligned on axis with the Jaffa gate, then opens out into a wide but enclosed paved court, passes into a larger triangular court planted with trees (pollarded for a shade canopy), and proceeds through a stone pergola with roof garden, onto the main stone plaza. This axial route continues visually through the main new building to the Russian compound beyond. The axis lies on an important ridge that approximates the old pilgrim and prophet's walk — *ha Nevi'im* — from the north. There is a Biblical account that says from a point on this ridge one could see the port of Acre. This was not believed until recently, when, on the demolition of a large building in that location, a distant view of Acre was revealed.

History and politics often expose divisive forces. The design challenge was to acknowledge both in ways that are inclusive and democratic. If these ancient issues can't (as yet) be resolved politically, then we can, at least, attempt to provide for them architecturally.

• • •

The success of the Jerusalem City Hall project led to an invitation to DSAI and Kolker Kolker Epstein to participate in a design competition for a new Foreign Ministry building, which we subsequently won. The site assigned to the new Ministry of Foreign Affairs was among the lesser government buildings surrounding the all-important Knesset, the supreme court building, and the Israel Museum. These are in a loose cluster on the National Boulevard.

We assumed three design objectives: the first was to add an aggregate to the lesser surrounding buildings in order to emphasize the importance of the three great institutions of state. Given the critical function of foreign affairs in Israel, however, the second objective was to also give a significance to the building itself. This was accomplished by aligning a part of the building with its neighbours and using a different geometry from the rest of the complex.

The final challenge was for the building to be as open and welcoming as possible — a symbol of a democratic society — yet have the necessary security. Like so much in Israel, there was the issue of reconciling two opposing perspectives.

In Israel, any unfamiliar building technology is tested at a bombing site in the desert. I had created a delicate onyx reception hall as the centrepiece of the complex, and it qualified as an unfamiliar technology. The first test forcefully demonstrated that, had it been built and subject to a rocket or cannon attack, it would have been an utter failure. We went back to the drawing board and found a way to preserve this delicate design feature while providing the necessary security. Out of adversity, invention: a staple of the country.

Jerusalem has a unique light, soft and expressive, and I wanted to take advantage of that in the design of the Foreign Ministry. Transparency in a building is a democratizing feature, while an opaque wall can imply totalitarianism. But the need for security in Israel is paramount. I was able to accommodate these opposing ideas by using translucent onyx walls in the main reception area, with a glass roof that is protected by a raised steel mesh parasol. The city's fabled light filters in, but the building is secure, and from the outside the building at night is a glowing beacon. Architecture is an ongoing attempt to reconcile often opposing forces: transparency and privacy, the individual and the collective, ambition and budget. Nowhere is this more apparent than in Israel.

. . .

While I was visiting the building site in 1997, the country essentially closed down. My Israeli colleagues' view was that the strike by the Histadrut, the umbrella union that closed the country down, was more political than economic. In any event, it left me stranded. The ports, airports, telephone systems, and municipal services were all shut down. There is always an air of tension in Israel, and being unable to get out left me with a sense of unease.

I therefore made reservations with British Airways to fly to London from Amman, then asked my client, the Foreign Office, to arrange passage for me to Amman via the Allenby Bridge, across the Jordan River. It was important to get to the bridge before it closed for the night if I was to catch my flight early the next morning. A trip to the frontier that normally takes about an hour from Jerusalem took thirty-eight minutes — a hair-raising drive through the Judean desert, past the Dead Sea, bypassing Jericho on new Israeli highways that were designed for strategic rather than ordinary-traffic purposes.

The frontier at night is a depressing affair. There are two fierce-looking checkpoints, fortified and bristling with the antennae of listening devices. We passed through the Israeli side effortlessly. After the checkpoint there were stark, utilitarian structures lit with overly bright fluorescent lights. A tough but kindly official escorted me through passport control to the other side. A van took me to the gate of the Allenby bridge, where an Israeli security agent walked my bag and me over the bridge. There is rigid control of vehicular traffic.

The vaunted bridge is an unimpressive structure — dilapidated and dusty steel truss sides, and a very uneven, unsecured plank roadbed. It is named after General Allenby, the British general who defeated the Turks in the First World War, a defeat that dismantled the last vestiges of the Ottoman Empire.

On the other side I was turned over to the Jordanian police and border officials. I was to have been met by a Jordanian-based Israeli Foreign Office car to drive me to Amman. Unfortunately, it had not yet appeared. I was taken into a seedy border post, where a thin, unshaven official in a poorly made uniform searched my Canadian passport for a visa, which I did not have. I suddenly remembered the scale models of Israeli tanks I had in my bag. The model maker who makes our architectural models in Jerusalem also makes precision models for the army. They use them for strategy sessions and to train soldiers in armour recognition. The model maker had made me a present of two of them, one being of the latest Merkava tank. I wondered how I would explain them to the border official if he were to search my bag. And I remembered, with some unease, a botched assassination attempt the previous month by two Israeli agents using false Canadian passports.

My driver finally arrived. He spoke little English, but a Jordanian American in the transit lounge translated. After several phone calls I was cleared and we drove off. As I began to relax, we drove into a more extensive Jordanian border control, where the driver disappeared with my passport into a building not dissimilar to its Israeli counterpart. As I waited in the car, I could see him going from desk to desk, then disappearing. Finally, a tall, lean, but muscular young man with close-cropped hair opened the door of the car and threw some gear in. He abruptly asked me to sit in the rear, explaining that he was a security agent who would protect me on the ride from the border to Amman. I noted the impressive bulge under his armpit. After an hour we arrived at the outskirts of Amman, and the security agent seemed to relax. He said the worst was over.

Amman has a curious city structure. Small apartment buildings with little relationship to the street or each other. I was among the first to arrive at the airport the next morning and it was with a profound sense of relief that I watched the desert recede as the aircraft rose, with my bag and undiscovered model tanks intact in the overhead bin.

. . .

On another trip to Israel, I was invited to join an Israeli entrepreneur and a Canadian railroad engineer to examine the feasibility of a railroad to link the Dead Sea with Eilat on the Red Sea. This was essentially to move potash for export. My task was to plan the route in Eilat so as to achieve the least disruption of the town's thriving tourist trade.

When we completed the analysis, we met with Prime Minister Begin. Begin seemed only mildly interested in the project. He was much more interested in whether a railroad linking Cairo to Tel Aviv might be equally feasible.

During the meeting, Begin surprised me by asking if I was Jewish. At first I thought he was joking with this old chestnut! But he was quite serious. When I affirmed that I was indeed Jewish, he rolled out yet another chestnut: "You don't look Jewish!"

. . .

The commissions in Israel necessitated frequent trips, and over the course of a decade I flew to Israel dozens of times. Sometimes, to vary the trip from the airport to Jerusalem, I would take the Modi'in Road through the West Bank. The road wends through hills of limestone terraces and olive groves, past cypress and pine and the sweet smell of honeysuckle. In the evening, the light, intense but soft, would illuminate the pale yellow stones and give the trees a glow.

Arab villages, their simple geometric buildings loosely but carefully grouped on hilltops, rested in the dusty greenery. Viewed from below no streets were visible. Man-made and natural forms combined in tranquility, the villages as perfectly composed as a fractured Cezanne landscape. Later, the outskirts of modern Jerusalem appeared in the fading, golden light, with new suburbs tightly clustered on hilltops. In this magical light both Arab villages and Israeli settlements concealed the conflicts that curse this land.

Seven

Caribbean Islands

OUR FIRST FAMILY HOLIDAY IN THE CARIBBEAN WAS LIT-erally a toss-up: we arrived at the airport without having decided whether to go to Cuba or Puerto Rico. We tossed a coin and Cuba won.

This was in 1976 and there were few vacation options in Cuba. Varadero Beach, once the holiday place of the Duponts, was one. Their mansion had been converted to a restaurant filled with pale-eyed Russians in cheap clothing. Presumably they were Party apparatchiks. They did not seem to be enjoying themselves, sitting in stolid silence. The headwaiter was a relic of the house's past, dressed in a white tuxedo with slicked back hair and a deferential manner that concealed his contempt.

We were given a cottage on the waterfront between the abandoned houses of former diplomats and the military airport. Fighter jets took off at all times of the day and night on their way to Angola, where the postcolonial left-wing government was successfully fighting South Africa. On Angola's eastern border with Mozambique, South Africa was also in a battle with Black guerillas. South African casualties were mounting. F.W. de Klerk, the South African president, was faced with two wars, internal opposition to apartheid, and growing international sanctions. A pragmatist, he began dismantling the apartheid government, enfranchising the Black population, and negotiating the transition with the jailed Nelson Mandela, who became the first Black president of South Africa.

The cottage we were assigned had no hot water, there were cockroaches nesting in light switches, and the bedsheets felt damp. I found a former diplomat's house that had a watchman who allowed me to fill a fire bucket with water, heat it on a gas stove, and rush over to the cottage with Gillian waiting in the bath. The food was limited — pork or fish for lunch and dinner every day — but the beach and swimming were good. We spotted Vo Nguyen Giap, I think it was, a victorious Vietnamese general enjoying some R and R in very friendly Cuba.

. . .

Eight years later, I went to Cuba with a group of Middle Eastern investors looking for real estate options. They had enlisted Eugene (Gene) Whelan, the minister of agriculture in Pierre Trudeau's cabinet, as a negotiator. Gene had a connection with Castro and Cuba. He persuaded me to accompany him to undertake any development that might ensue. Gene was a large man, both physically and politically, and invariably wore a large, green Stetson. He was a colourful character. He once said, "Canada has two official languages and I don't speak none of them." He was very popular in Cuba, having defeated the U.S. government's attempts to prevent Cuba becoming a member of the UN Food and Agriculture organization, and providing Cuba with breeding bulls from Canada. Fidel once visited the bulls with Gene, and put his arm around one of them, claiming it was his best friend.

The hotel we stayed in was not much better than the one in Varadero Beach. Gene complained about his shower, which produced only a trickle of water. At breakfast the next day, Gene said he'd had a visitor at about midnight. It was Fidel, who said, "I understand you are having trouble with your shower!"

Any development by the Middle Eastern investors hinged on their being able to own the land. When it became clear that the prohibition on owning land was not negotiable, the delegation gave up its Cuban ambitions and we all went home.

• • •

A third trip to Cuba promised a more positive outcome. Ian Delaney, a successful Toronto broker, had invested heavily in Cuba, in soybean production, and he had the cellphone monopoly. The Helms-Burton legislation in the U.S. had Ian firmly in mind when it banned those with connections in Cuba from coming into the U.S. As a result, he no longer had access to his vacation house in Florida.

When the Russians withdrew from Cuba, Ian offered to take over the oil sector, which they had previously run. In his proposal to Fidel, Ian claimed he could improve production by 20 percent. Fidel was skeptical, but Ian did improve it by at least that amount. He also strengthened his ties to Cuba by appointing some Cubans to the boards of his Canadian enterprises.

Havana is a very beautiful city, but was in decay from a lack of maintenance. This was caused in part by the priority given to education and the excellent universal health care system. Fidel said to Ian, "You are my favourite capitalist. You have benefitted from your investments in Cuba. You should now invest in the real estate of Cuba." So Ian asked me to come to Cuba to investigate potential real estate investment.

On that trip, I had the pleasure of staying in what was once a Spanish nobleman's Havana townhouse, just off Plaza Viejo. Now a small boutique hotel, the Hotel Santa Isabel Habana, it had been constructed not long after the establishment of Havana in the sixteenth century.

Cuba has some of the best beaches in the Caribbean, and my first priority was to review beach sites for vacation tourism. I rented a Russian-made helicopter for this survey. It was so big it had large armchairs in the cabin, as well as an air hostess. I asked her for a teaspoon to stir my tea as we took off. She replied that I didn't need one; the vibration of the craft would be enough. Which turned out to be true.

At one particularly attractive location, I asked the pilot to land so I could take a closer look at the site. He landed on a steeply sloped sand dune, and I complimented him on his capability. He replied that it was pretty easy if you weren't being shot at. He had been in the Cuban Air Force in Angola.

Ian noted that whatever beach location I picked, it would not prevent a competitor from becoming a neighbour.

Thereafter I concentrated on the choice sites in the city. There were three good candidates, one a quarry close to what had been the Hilton hotel in the newer sector of the city, and two in the old city, one a former bank and the other derelict.

We developed preliminary designs for these three sites and I called a meeting with Havana's chief planner. He arrived with the whole planning department, some forty people. I found it hard to imagine what occupied such a large staff, given the very low level of development in the city.

It became clear that they had little experience in the planning approval process. The chief planner began to make his own proposals, which only demonstrated his lack of experience, or an understanding of even the most fundamental aspects of what was required for office space or hotels. There was no systematic planning approval process with a reasonably predictable schedule. Given the unreliability of the power supply, sewage system, and water supply, any development would need to provide its own emergency power, sewage, and water systems. The state would still have ownership of the land, while Ian would be paying taxes, maintenance, and interest on borrowed capital. With much regret, I recommended that Ian not take on any development. As much as I would have liked to work in Cuba, it didn't make sense. Havana puts any Florida town to shame, and the Cubans are a lively, sympatico people, but the development had too many hurdles. So ended my professional engagement in the most interesting city and island in the Caribbean.

• • •

Gillian and I continued to explore the Caribbean for our winter holidays. In each island we visited, I would check out sites on which we might build a holiday house. In 1987, Gillian saw an ad in the *Financial Times* for the sale of a house on Mustique. The island seemed to me the very antithesis of a place for a relaxed, informal vacation. Originally owned by an eccentric British aristocrat, Lord Glenconner, it had British royalty and a rock star among its homeowners. I feared the island would be a cozy club for the RAF (the rich and famous).

Friends who were familiar with the island encouraged us nonetheless to take a look. When we arrived on Mustique, our first impression was that the description of the property, with the typical estate agent's gloss, was far more attractive than the place itself. We were, however, pleasantly surprised at the informality of the island, and the very warm welcome we were given by the few homeowners we met. An important factor in Mustique's favour was that the island was owned by the homeowners, and, unlike almost every other Caribbean island, it was consequently secure. The island was governed by a board of elected homeowners and run, for the most part, by Vincentians. At that time, there were a number of sites for sale. Brian Alexander, managing director, toured the island with us.

The early settlement on Mustique was predominantly on the Caribbean side of the island. Since the ocean was calmer, the hotel, shops, and wharf were sited there. The Atlantic side, despite its stunning fine coral sand beaches, was thought too windy and the ocean too rough to render development attractive. We looked at sites on both sides. One site on the Atlantic coast had been put up for sale by Cheryl Tiegs, an actress/model, and her husband, Peter Beard, the wildlife photographer. On our visit, I noted that a heavily treed promontory provided a natural wind buffer to the site. It also had the advantage of being on a kilometre-long beach and, even better, bordered a vast conservation area. No other building would be visible from the property. We bought it, and I set about designing our Caribbean holiday home, which was to be named Simplicity.

The Caribbean has climatic conditions similar to those in South Africa. The first building I designed, in 1958, was a restaurant in Durban. In subtropical Durban, two pressing design issues are heat gain and occasional rain deluges. I designed a delicate repetitive concrete barrel roof, two and a half inches thick at the apexes, and seven inches in the valleys, which provided shade. A sliding glass enclosure afforded cross ventilation, and projecting barrel vaults gave rain protection.

My design for Simplicity honoured the principles of passive environmental modification. The aim was to achieve comfortable temperatures without the use of air conditioning, and to collect rainwater for irrigation and bathing. I designed the house with double ventilated roof structures, through-room ventilation, and south shading. The bedrooms were well separated, each with its own private veranda and outdoor shower.

At the time, very few building supplies were available locally in Mustique. I spent a great deal of time acquiring what was needed to construct the house and shipping materials to Mustique: concrete block from Trinidad, wood from Guyana, sand from Saint Vincent, and steel reinforcing from Barbados.

We moved into Simplicity for Christmas 1990. Our move was not exactly smooth. On Christmas Eve our range and refrigerator were hastily dumped on the wharf so the vessel that brought them from St. Vincent could help a yacht wedged on the Montezuma ledge. Our son Andrew and a crew of helpers delivered the appliances at midnight. I promptly plugged the 110-volt range and oven into Mustique's 220-volt power supply. That concluded the short life of our stove. A typical Mustique story.

. . .

As a consequence of the success of Simplicity, I have, over the years, taken on the design and supervised the construction of three other houses on Mustique: Indigo, Alumbrera, and Taliesin. All were designed with passive means of tempering the environment for human comfort.

. . .

Not long after we established ourselves on Mustique, I was elected to the board of the Mustique Company, which effectively runs the island, and charged with drawing up a master plan.

In the nineteenth century, sugar and cotton plantations had been established on Mustique by two families, the Macks and the Rooneys (hence the naming of "Macaroni" beach). Neither prospered, and locals established ownership by eminent domain. Lord Glenconner then bought the island in the late 1950's.

Early settlement on Mustique had primarily been along the Caribbean coast, both for shipping safety and convenience. This pattern was continued in its first modern redevelopment: the old cotton barn was converted to the public spaces of the Cotton House Hotel, and the first new houses were constructed in the same vicinity. Around the wharf, retail uses as well as a restaurant followed. Mechanical maintenance services and the first primitive general store were in fairly close proximity, along with a village and a church for local inhabitants. The sole planning document regulating the island's development at this time was a density calculation directly related to the size of the site involved.

I developed a master plan where existing land uses were formalized, and limits put on expansion. For the south end of the island I devised lots separated by company-owned corridors that would provide privacy for future houses, but also produce a web of pedestrian paths across the island.

After the construction of four houses at the south end of the island, as set out in the new master plan, the board, with my full support, decided to revert to the status quo ante: that is, to keep the natural landscape undeveloped. Most islands obliterate the very aspects that attracted development in the first place. Mustique was determined not to make the same mistake.

Not selling more lots on the undeveloped south end of the island might have been perceived as forfeiting a prime source of revenue. I noted, however, that this did not necessarily mean a reduction of income: demand for a desirable product in short supply inevitably leads to higher prices. Preserving the character of the island by avoiding overdevelopment, and maintaining large swaths of the natural landscape, enhanced the attraction of the island.

As Mustique is privately owned (home owners are given the opportunity to purchase shares in the island ownership), it had the power to determine the extent of development. This included the construction of an airstrip deliberately limited in runway length to prevent access by large jets. There is also a limit to the size of ships that can access the island, avoiding large tour vessels and their enormous passenger loads.

• • •

Simplicity has been an anchor for my family. Some of our grandchildren have moved house, even countries, a number of times, but that house has been a constant. For decades, Simplicity has played a significant role in our family — a happy, relaxed haven where we could all get together. It is hard to imagine a better sanctuary than Mustique: individual independence and collective control; a blissful climate with a fertile, verdant natural environment; a secure oasis in a turbulent world; and the prevalence of peace and quiet.

Eight

Acoustical Variations

IN 1997, CANADA WAS WITHOUT A MODERN OPERA HOUSE. The only purpose-built opera house — the Grand Opera House in Toronto — had been demolished in 1927. Richard Bradshaw, conductor of the Canadian Opera Company's (COC's) orchestra and its artistic director, likened the effort to get an opera house built in Toronto to the Thirty Years' War in Europe (1618–48). Though less bloody, the opera house battle took almost as long. It began in the 1980s, when Hal Jackman, president of the Ballet Opera House Corporation, lobbied for a new building to replace what was then named the O'Keefe Centre (later the Hummingbird Centre, the Sony Centre, now Meridian Hall) in which the COC had performed since 1960. Before that, opera had been performed in the Royal Alexandra and the Elgin Theatres.

In 1984, Ontario Premier Bill Davis set aside a downtown lot that was intended to be the site for a new opera
house. A design competition was held and subsequently won
by Moshe Safdie. The project received approval in 1988, and
the buildings on the site were demolished in preparation.
The estimated construction cost was $311 million. Two years
later, Bob Rae was elected as premier, inheriting a substantial
deficit. At the time, the province was also dealing with the
$570 million cost of the Skydome, the new venue to house
sporting events (originally budgeted at $150 million, it was
sold in 2004 to Rogers Communications for $25 million, or
roughly four percent of construction costs, a disaster on every
level). The Rae government asked Safdie and the board for a
more modest design to bring the costs down. They refused to
comply, and in 1992 the province cancelled the project and
sold the land to developers.

In 1997, the project was revived. This time the site was a
courthouse building and parking lot at the corner of University
Avenue and Queen Street. Originally, the idea was to incorpor-
ate an office and condominium tower to be built by Olympia
and York, which would help fund the cost of the opera house.
Christopher Ondaatje, the London financier, also agreed to
donate $20 million. Both parties eventually withdrew their
support, and Toronto Mayor Mel Lastman refused to provide
any municipal funds.

Nevertheless, Richard Bradshaw pressed on. In 2002, he
announced an architectural competition. Ten firms submitted proposals, and these were whittled down to four finalists, Diamond Schmitt among them. The Board of the COC
formed a committee, which spent half a day or more in the
offices of each of the four finalists. We spent considerable time

and effort on the presentation to the committee and prepared ourselves for the questions they would inevitably ask.

We won the competition, but not everyone was happy with the choice. A small group that included Murray Frum, a dentist turned developer, and Larry Richards, chair of the Faculty of Architecture at University of Toronto, who should have known better, and a few others, approached Bradshaw and the board with an appeal to appoint Frank Gehry as architect for the project. Bradshaw told them that a Gehry design would most likely carry a premium cost (the Safdie design had been almost double the cost of ours), and, as the budget was tight, would the group provide a million dollars to cover the extra cost? The group faded, and we heard no more of them.

The principle we followed, indeed one we always follow, was to first identify the objectives of the project, then to demonstrate how these would be met. The central objectives on this project were the acoustics, audience comfort, and back-of-house efficiency. Such an approach is the opposite to that of architects who first design an attractive form, and then give it to the acoustician to address the sound requirements. The Sydney Opera House is an iconic design that has brought a great deal of attention to the city, and to opera in Australia, but as Bradshaw said, "it's a dreadful house inside." Designing from the outside results in concert spaces that may have curb appeal, but often have poor acoustics and unfortunate sightlines. We designed from both the inside out — consulting extensively with acousticians — and from the outside in — creating a design that also took its context into account.

Opera is viewed as a rarified, elite art, and was in grave danger of losing audience share partly because of that. It was critical to make the Opera House accessible — in both physical and psychological terms. Facing University Avenue, a main thoroughfare, we created a completely transparent facade. The transparency of the public areas, making the public areas an extension of the city, was intended to democratize the institution. Even during the day, passers-by can see inside. The lobby is used for receptions, and the Richard Bradshaw Amphitheatre, a multipurpose space that holds a hundred free concerts a year, is visible from University Avenue. At night, the lit interior acts as a beacon. Those who are attending the opera proceed from the expansive, urban experience of the lobbies that look out to the city, to the contrasting, contained, and intimate interior of the auditorium.

While the transparency of the design of the lobbies was a priority, we were faced with the problem of an all-glass facade facing west. Without some form of shading the lobbies would be unbearably hot on sunny days. We designed a series of roller shades. When furled, their small-diameter housings would not obscure the view, either externally or from within. When they are unfurled, by a thermostatic trigger, the facade looks like a clipper ship in full sail.

The groundbreaking ceremony for what was now officially named the Four Seasons Centre for the Performing Arts was in April 2003. Bradshaw had planned for Wagner's Ring Cycle — four works, four directors, fifteen hours of opera — to open the new building in the fall of 2006. Preparing a prodction of that scale and ambition takes almost as much planning and as many people as it takes to design and build an opera house. So the usual pressures of time and budget were heightened.

When we excavated the site we found that the subsoil clay carried sound wonderfully, which created a problem as the University Avenue subway runs parallel to the site. This meant

extra care in providing sound attenuation measures. We needed
to achieve an N1 rating, that is, no external sound discernable
to the human ear, inside the auditorium. The excavation also
came across water and storm pipes that the city's plan showed
would be outside the boundaries of our site. They weren't.
Clearly, the city's plans were at fault. However, the city declined to accept the cost of moving the pipes.

To ensure an N1 rating we rested the superstructure on 489
rubber pads sandwiched between large blocks of the concrete
foundation and the opera house structure. This isolation device
was also employed on all vertical and horizontal surfaces of
the building's external envelope. The house itself is a structure
within a structure, with no rigid connection between the two.
Sound attenuation is achieved by both mass and discontinuity
— heavy concrete for defence against low-frequency sound,
and discontinuity for high-frequency sound. As a result, we
achieved the N1 rating.

But those measures only dealt with noise, not acoustics.
The quality of the acoustics are determined by the shape of
the room, the texture of the surfaces of the enclosure, and the
configuration of the walls, balcony fronts, and ceilings. Low,
medium, and high frequencies need to be blended and reflected
equally to every seat.

A concert hall and its acoustics were the subject of my
Bachelor of Architecture thesis: which meant I knew that I
had to have an excellent acoustician. Russell Johnson had a
great reputation as an acoustician, and he was appointed to the
project. I met him in New York to make the point that I wanted to work *with* the acoustician, not to have a solution imposed
on us without collaboration. Johnson assured me this would be
the case. Then he provided a design without any consultation.

When I expressed concern, he replied that this was the way it was to be.

Johnson seldom came to Toronto to attend project meetings, sending a junior instead. At a fairly advanced stage, when we had begun the construction drawings, we were given the message from Johnson, via the junior, that we should add another balcony to the auditorium. The board agreed with me he should be fired. He was unable to collaborate, unable to provide an explanation of acoustic principles so I could interpret them in creatively appropriate forms, and his lack of input at the earlier stages was unprofessional.

We then retained Bob Essert of Sound Space Design, who was good to work with. He would engage in discussion about shape, texture, and detail configurations of every surface. We held a series of acoustic tests. By allowing the physics of sound to generate the design, the volume, configuration, materials, and surface textures, we hoped to have at least an 80 percent success. Tests revealed that it was 90 percent, which meant that the final 10 percent could be achieved by tuning the hall with minor adjustments. In instances where the form of the house is predetermined by the architect, and then given to the acoustician to fix, at best it will probably never exceed a 60 percent acoustic success ratio.

Various audiences filled the room for the tests. We produced a full range of sound, from the lowest to the highest frequencies. We tested solo musical instruments and then a full orchestra, from Mozart (with a small number of players), to Wagner (with a mammoth orchestra), along with vocal soloists and full choirs. During the last test a full orchestra played a wide variety of pieces from the opera repertoire. At the end of the concert, Richard Bradshaw left the pit with his hand shielding his eyes.

He was in tears at the perfection of the acoustics. The first violinist said he didn't know his instrument could sound that way. The acoustics rank among the best in the world.

The auditorium is in the traditional European horseshoe design, with five levels of shallow balconies. It is a bare twenty-eight metres wide, with the first row of balconies only twenty-seven metres from the stage. As a result, almost 75 percent of the seats are within thirty metres of centre stage. The horseshoe design invites an intimacy — the audience sees itself, and watches and responds as a collective. The orchestra pit is intimate, yet large enough to accommodate Wagner's oversized works.

As we did with our architectural team, Bradshaw started with a small, core group. As the building and the opera began to take shape, hundreds more people were added — acousticians, engineers, soloists, tuba players. There are groupies who attend Wagner's Ring Cycle wherever it is performed in the world. This would be a test of the building.

The result was glorious — both the building and the production were praised, the acoustics singled out for their clarity. In the previous O'Keefe Centre, the Canadian Opera Company had had difficulty attracting singers and directors to Toronto. Those who did come were sometimes reluctant to return. The new building has had no difficulty attracting the best performers. When Alexander Neef, who had been casting director of the Paris opera, became the artistic director of the Four Seasons, he said it was because of the building.

• • •

We employed the same principles when designing la Maison symphonique de Montréal. The competition was a P3 process — bidding to design, finance, build, and operate, the first for an arts building. The client was the Province of Quebec, which did not just set performance guidelines, but offered its own design solutions. We retained our own acoustician and vibration engineers to see if we could improve the prescribed solutions.

The site was above a parking garage for Place des Arts. The design solution offered by the province designated a three-metre buffer between the auditorium and the parking structure below to achieve the required sound attenuation. Three metres of a building's height represents a considerable cost. Using the California vibration engineers we'd used on the Four Seasons Centre, we found a way to achieve the same resistance to vibration with just one metre of depth. This also allowed us to put the loading dock at stage level. That meant the province would enjoy not just a saving in capital costs, but in operating costs, as well. This cost factor added to the success of our proposed design, and we won the competition.

One of the design objectives for the auditorium was to have a consistent and complete envelopment of the space — in a sense the contemporary equivalent to the cohesion Baroque architecture achieved, which included every aspect of the architecture. The Montreal auditorium was to include an organ. A standard organ design would, however, introduce an alien element whose design would be based on conventional organ arrangements — which, in my view, was the equivalent of a giant radiator.

Fortunately Casavant, an organ maker of global significance, is located in Saint-Hyacinthe, not far from Montreal. I arranged to meet with their craftsmen to discuss the design of the organ. And, happily, they agreed to work with me on the project.

The organ in question, le Grand Orgue Pierre-Béique, consists of 83 stops, 116 ranks and a phenomenal 6,489 pipes. Only a fraction of these are seen in the auditorium. I sketched an asymmetric disposition of the visible pipes in the same design language as the rest of the auditorium, with an acoustically transparent screen behind them concealing the majority of the pipes. In this way, the organ became a harmonious focal point.

Thus, la Maison symphonique achieves design cohesion of its diverse elements, together with exacting acoustics. When competing to renovate the symphony hall in Lincoln Centre in New York, to be known as Geffen Hall, members of the selection committee visited the concert hall in Montreal. One of them simply said, "This is what we want."

. . .

Architects are usually selected prior to the selection of acousticians and theatre consultants for performing-arts projects. However, in the case of the Buddy Holly Hall of Performing Arts and Sciences, the acousticians and theatre specialists had already been retained.

We were on the shortlist of architects to design the centre in Buddy Holly's hometown of Lubbock, Texas, a city of 250,000 inhabitants. The intention was to provide a 2,000 seat main hall, a 450-seat chamber theatre, a school band competition space, and a ballet school. The board, which also acted as the architect selection committee, had also previously appointed two local architectural firms to work with the winning architecture firm.

During our interview, a member of the selection committee asked if we had seen a brochure from Nieman Marcus, which included an image of the Toronto opera house. They asked whether we knew of Nieman Marcus, the Dallas department store. I replied, did she mean "Needless Markup"? The selection committee broke up in laughter, and an architect from one of the local firms leaned over the conference table and shook my hand. At times, big decisions can turn on seemingly inconsequential factors: we won the project by a unanimous vote.

For our presentation to the board, we wanted to demonstrate our open-minded approach to design by illustrating three generically different schemes. This allowed the client to participate in the design process, discussing the merits of each approach. Don Schmitt, Matthew Lella, and I each developed a scheme for discussion. The board settled on a scheme I'd created where the constituent parts were grouped around a common lobby space. This accomplished both a separate identity for each component in a dynamic relation to the others, and also a cohesive result.

. . .

A member of the selection committee commented later that it was not only our success with large projects that had impressed the board, but also our success with smaller ones. A much smaller project was to follow the Buddy Holly.

. . .

At a dinner party in Mustique in 2015, I was seated next to Tania Freeman. The conversation began with the usual exploratory questions about where one lived and one's occupation. She is an ex-barrister who was then engaged in interior design, living in London with children attending Marlborough College. At some point, the conversation turned to design and architecture, and to my long-standing interest in acoustics and concert halls.

Several weeks later, Tania called me. She had been asked by Marlborough College to provide them with a shortlist of architects to refurbish and reconfigure their historic Memorial Hall. The small performing-arts hall, she explained, was a living memorial to the 749 young Marlburians who had lost their lives in the First World War. My interest was piqued, and since I was to be in the U.K. shortly thereafter, I suggested that I take a look at the project.

The Hall was in a bad state of repair, and I could immediately see the challenges the semicircular auditorium posed to the acoustics. It also suffered from a lack of back-of-house facilities and a paucity of audience amenities. Neither performers nor spectators were well served.

The hall's greatest deficiency was its abysmal acoustics. The semicircular form focused sound in one central location, and the hard wall surfaces produced a reverberation time that was far too long, rendering speech almost unintelligible. I was immediately reminded of Hunt Hall (formerly the Fogg Museum) at Harvard, a room with a very similar semicircular configuration, where acoustics were just as problematic. Indeed, it was at Hunt Hall, in the late nineteenth century, that the science of room acoustics was developed. The president of the university asked a physicist, Wallace Clement Sabine, to see what he could do to improve speech intelligibility in the hall. Sabine established the appropriate reverberation times (the length of time that sound is audible between production and decay) for different categories of sound: short (under one second) for speech and chamber music; medium (between one and two seconds) for symphonic music; and long (over two seconds) for organ music. In fact, it was Sabine who defined reverberation time. Later, as a result of his seminal work, Sabine was retained as a consultant for the Boston Symphony Hall, the first concert hall to be designed with acoustics as a key factor. The BSH is today generally still considered to be among the best symphony halls, acoustically. Sabine was given the honour of having the unit of sound absorption named after him.

After my first meeting with the staff at Marlborough College, I was asked if I would take on the project myself, and I agreed.

During the time we were working on the renovation of the Hall, Peter and Tania Freeman generously provided accommodation at their House on the Hill. The Freemans had acquired some old farm buildings, the only buildings in a vast agricultural area, and Tania had done a superb job of converting the buildings to a wonderful country retreat.

The budget for Memorial Hall was small, and resolving the acoustical problems was my highest priority. I got in touch with acousticians with whom I had worked, who happily took on the project. To resolve the challenge within budget, the stage was expanded while keeping the structural support of the proscenium arch. Matthew Lella of DSAI added a highly articulated reflective ceiling over the stage with a pattern inspired by the mathematical Penrose tile based on pentagons. This, and the addition of convex hinged panels across the rear wall of the auditorium, resolved the acoustical issues. We also reconfigured the internal space in a way that created more back-of-house room as well as better audience facilities below the auditorium.

Following a series of BBC concerts recorded at the renovated Hall, Phillip Dukes, the head of the music faculty at Marlborough College, who is also the first violinist in the London Symphony Orchestra, pronounced it one of the finest chamber music halls in the U.K.

. . .

An even smaller structure with its own acoustic challenges was to come. I met a friend of Yvonne and Pierre Winkler at the opening of the Harman Center in Washington, D.C., which I had designed for the Shakespeare company. Apparently, the Winklers planned to sell their house in London and retire to Switzerland, Pierre being Swiss and Yvonne German. They were therefore looking for an architect to design a house for them in Zurich, and a dinner was arranged in London for me to meet them.

They told me about their aims for their proposed Zurich house, and I accepted the commission. It is a principle I have always maintained that the client provides every requirement — that is, the program of accommodation, and particularly their life style — but not their aesthetic preferences. The architect has to exercise his or her psychological skills to discern the clients' often unstated values and ambitions.

Here, considerations included the fact that Pierre and his family once owned a trading company in China, and, as a consequence, he had acquired a significant collection of Chinese art and sculpture which would need to be properly exhibited in the new house. There was also a desire for a large garage to accommodate Pierre's sizable car collection. And, with Yvonne's keen interest in music, she asked that the living room be designed to accommodate chamber music.

Working in Switzerland, I discovered that the Swiss, unsurprisingly, not only have rigid rules governing the permissible amount of floor space for houses in any given location, but also rules relating to the configuration of the building. In Zurich, we needed to maintain the outline of a traditional Swiss house, with two storeys above grade and a pitched roof. Furthermore, neighbours are empowered to voice their opinions, and the framework of any proposed structure is erected on site for neighbours' consideration. Fortunately, we encountered no objections.

In addition to designing the space to display the Chinese collection, and a large subterranean garage, I designed the living room, per Yvonne's wish, with suitable acoustics for chamber music performances.

Handel understood acoustics. He forbade the dusting of columns, walls, and balcony fronts of the halls he was to play in. Dust refracts high-frequency sound, the garlands and putti decoration of balcony fronts in classical halls refract medium frequencies, and the shaped balcony fronts, low-frequency sounds. Together, the result is a balanced sound, incorporating the full spectrum of frequencies.

Originally, rooms within palaces where concerts played would have had carpets on the floors, tapestries on the walls, and heavy drapery on the windows. All these furnishings are highly sound absorptive; hence, chamber music, from the seventeenth to nineteenth centuries, was designed for circumstances with short reverberation times. Clearly, not all of those components are appropriate in a contemporary home. So, in the Winkler's living room, the wood panelling is finely perforated to produce the required short reverberation time.

Both our associate Swiss architect, Anders Kuechel, and the contractor, who worked with Swiss precision, were of the highest standard. It was a pleasure all round: the project, client, associate architect, and contractor.

Nine

Architecture Competitions

THE FIRST KNOWN ARCHITECTURE COMPETITION WAS born of disaster. When the Persian King Xerxes invaded Athens in the fifth century BCE, he destroyed many of the Greek buildings. After Xerxes was driven out, a competition was held to design a suitable victory monument. A local architect won, and his design was fashioned from the rubble of the Temple of Athena and built on the grounds of the Acropolis.

During the Renaissance, the practice was revived, and the architects who won competitions tended to receive favour from religious or political figures. Sometimes this formula was reversed and a favoured architect won the competition regardless of merit. In the 1490s Florence needed a new council hall in what is now known as the Palazzo Vecchio. A number of artists and architects were in competition for the project, among them Leonardo da Vinci. The project was awarded to Simone del Pollaiuolo, however, who was a friend and follower of Savonarola, ruler of Florence at the time. Savonarola was hanged and burned in front of the Palazzo a few years later, though not for choosing the wrong architect.

Modern competitions generally produce publicity and spark public debate on design, which can be a good thing. They also raise the profile of the winning architect, a double-edged sword that has led to the concept of celebrity architecture. Many of the world's most prominent modern buildings are the result of an architectural competition.

However, there are few professional standards for competitions. There have been selection committees with no architect members — the equivalent of having illiterates determine a literary prize. It means few members of the jury are able to interpret design intent. There are juries dominated by a single member, who effectively determines the winner. Competitions can be beauty pageants where the most dramatic, eye-catching design wins, regardless of how impractical it is, or how expensive, or how it has failed to address fundamental design challenges. Or how it fits into the given site. The envelope of the building should not be a Procrustean bed into which the functions are forced. If the envelope is designed to accommodate the internal functions, its content can be reflected by form, material, and fenestration, among other elements to be read externally; the opposite of a Procrustean bed. But this isn't always a consideration with competitions.

Competitions can be corrupt, with a largely predetermined winner, the rest of the field reduced to also-rans, though giving the semblance of competition. Whatever else competitions are, they are certainly expensive for those who enter them. The first stage, where credentials are submitted, has a relatively small cost. But the next stage, the actual design stage, can have a huge cost, depending on submission requirements. This means that models, renderings, videos, and drawings have to be produced. Whether done in-house or not, these can amount to thousands of dollars. For major projects they can amount to $100,000, or more. It is rare that the honorarium paid to the shortlisted finalists comes anywhere close to covering costs.

Competitions conducted by what is known as the P3 system (public-private partnership), in which the submission is made by consortia consisting of design, build, finance, and maintenance companies, are even more onerous. In order to submit a financial package — the cost of construction and maintenance — a detailed set of construction drawings needs to be produced to accurately assess costs. The P3 system simply adds to those costs (the *Globe and Mail* has estimated that the P3 system adds 16 percent) and is quite unnecessary.

For the losing firms in an architectural competition, there is not just the expense, but the lost productivity. In addition to the costs borne by the competing companies, the government body administering the competition often adds a further cost as an entry fee, sometimes equivalent to the architect's fee. Such expenses effectively limit the vast majority of firms from competing.

Competitions can be undemocratic, expensive, and arbitrary, but in the quest for major projects they are often the only game in town. Of course, one's perspective shifts if one wins.

. . .

In January 2015, David Cameron, the British prime minister, announced that there would be a new U.K. Holocaust memorial and learning centre to be built in central London. The project had a budget of $165 million. The architectural competition was international and open to everyone. There were ninety-two entries and there was to be a shortlist of six. The shortlist was then expanded to ten, which was a surprise. Generally, shortlists get shorter, not longer. The ostensible reason was that the superb quality of the entrants demanded a longer shortlist. All ten of us on it were invited to submit designs.

The central challenge for a Holocaust memorial is, once again, how to reconcile two opposing forces — the descent into unimaginable horror and the humanity that survived and thrived in the wake of that horror. Architecturally, there is the need for restraint, while at the same time creating a memorable form. We started with a fundamental question: How does one give justice to the memory of the innocent millions who lost their lives?

Our response was a memorial that was designed not just to be observed, but to be experienced. As visitors descended a helical ramp, they would pass cast-iron walls textured with a bas-relief of six million rectangular nuggets. The descent took visitors into the Court of Conscience, which was open to the sky with a view of the Houses of Parliament's Victoria Tower, a symbol of democracy and tolerance. The decreasing amount of light as the visitor descended into the memorial itself was in contrast to the natural light above. There was no need for an extravagant structure, as the Holocaust is of such horrific magnitude itself. Instead, we wanted to convey the presence of absence. We wanted a combination of darkness and light, reflecting opposing forces. For, as Anne Michaels writes in her novel *Fugitive Pieces*, "there's nothing a man will not do to another, nothing a man will not do for another."

Among the fifteen jury members were the mayor of London, Sadiq Khan, and the city's chief rabbi, Ephraim Mirvis. Only one juror was an architect. Formal presentations of the short-listed work took place in the auditorium of the Victoria and Albert Museum and the event was open to the public. We were each given thirty minutes to explain our schemes.

Most of the jury were present, but at our presentation Mayor Sadiq Khan and two other jurors were missing. The final presentation, at which the selection committee was to make its decision, took place in the Admiralty building off Whitehall. Without warning, we were given only five minutes to recap our schemes. Kahn and the other two members of the jury who had been absent from the first presentation were in attendance. They had missed the main presentation when we had explained our concept and the thinking behind it in detail, yet they retained their right to vote.

As mayor of London, Kahn had appointed prominent local architects as ambassadors to London's municipalities to give opinions regarding development proposals that might not conform to code or zoning ordinance, but might be worth pursuing. One of those ambassadors was British-Ghanian architect David Adjaye, who was also one of the ten finalists. In the end it was Adjaye who won, with Diamond Schmitt receiving a special mention from the jury.

The link between the winning architect and the mayor, presumably a powerful figure on the jury, was unfortunate. As in law, it is best if architectural competitions avoid even the appearance of bias or ethical compromise. Our design, I felt, was my best work. It solved every problem that had been set out in the competition brief, as well as problems that hadn't been anticipated. To lose a competition can be heartbreaking. It isn't just the imagining of the building in its totality that is lost, but the imagining of the impact on society it would have had.

. . .

The U.K. Holocaust Memorial wasn't the first competition to leave a sour taste. In 2002, an international competition for a new museum complex at Yad Vashem was announced. The original Yad Vashem Museum began construction in 1954 on the Mount of Remembrance in Jerusalem. It was Israel's official Holocaust memorial, dedicated to preserving the memory of the six million dead and honouring those who fought the Nazis. It first opened to the public in 1957.

In 1993 plans began for a new, more technologically sophisticated museum on the site. Almost a decade later, an international competition yielded a shortlist of ten firms, ours among them. Our scheme gave a sense of the magnitude of the Shoa with a memorial avenue of a thousand columns, each with six thousand names on it.

The competition was presented as a two-stage process, and after the first stage, six firms were eliminated. We were among the remaining four firms. We presented our design to the selection committee where it was received with applause, the first time that has happened to us in a competition. To our surprise, we were subsequently told there would now be a third stage. Moshie Safdie, the Canadian-Israeli architect, who had been eliminated in the first stage, magically reappeared on the list for this third stage. Safdie won.

Again, the circumstances of the competition were muddy and, at best, idiosyncratic. It is never a joy to lose a competition — all that work and planning to conceive something that is stillborn. But the slightest hint of favouritism or cronyism diminishes the competition itself as well as those who have participated.

· · ·

Occasionally, competitions backfire. The 1983 competition for a new opera house in Paris attracted 744 entries, eventually winnowed to a shortlist of three. French president François Mitterrand had designated a new opera house as one of his *Grands Projets*. It was a blind competition; the names of the architects weren't attached to their work. Mitterand and his aides chose a design they were convinced had been done by American architect Richard Meier. They wanted the democratic stamp of a blind competition, but they also wanted a marquee name. They were devastated to find out that the design they chose hadn't been done by Meier, but by Carlos Ott, a Uruguayan-born architect who at the time was working for a large developer in Toronto. Ott's design was built amid the kind of controversy at which the French excel.

Ten

A Greater Cause

TECHNOLOGICALLY, WE CAN NOW BUILD ANYTHING WE can conceive of, and this is a mixed blessing. In his book *Architecture Without Architects,* Bernard Rudofsky writes of how creative and efficient indigenous architecture can be, an architecture born of necessity that adapts brilliantly to the climate. Perhaps the most dramatic example is the igloo. Snow and ice, not friendly materials for humans, are fashioned into a structure of great strength and high wind resistance, essentially a three-dimensional arch. Like an arch, the more pressure exerted on it, the tighter it holds together. And the thick walls offer insulation.

In the hot, dry climate of desert environments, the diurnal range is great, with hot days and a very bright sun contrasted with cool nights. The available building materials are limited to sand and clay. Thick mud walls are slow to heat up during the day and slow to cool during the cold nights. Small windows minimize glare and interior heating.

The economy of means that has determined architecture throughout history, and has given us ingenious structures born of necessity, has largely disappeared. Now we can build anything, anywhere. Unfortunately, we often do. Architecture is too often unconnected to local climate and urban context. It ignores its site and the programs it contains. There is an arrogance to many modern structures — from suburban houses to urban condominiums to museums. It is an arrogance that is out of step with this moment in history when climate change and environmental degradation are presenting all too real consequences.

Climate change presents many challenges, including economic; it may result in the greatest market failure in history. If we proceed with business as usual, it will cost us economically, socially, morally, and, of gravest concern, existentially. In 1961 there were three billion people in the world, and we used half the resources — food, water, arable land, energy — that the planet could sustainably provide. In 1986 there were five billion people and we consumed all the sustainable resources. For thirty-five years, we have been running a deficit.

The only effective way to combat climate change is to reduce our carbon intensity to zero. Among the effective ways of achieving that are the careful planning of cities and the design of buildings. The case for an architecture that is environmentally sustainable has never been stronger. The moral debate hasn't resulted in much progress; the financial case may win more converts. Indeed, clients are increasingly demonstrating a willingness to explore green technologies if it will save them money.

Currently, the capital cost of building a completely sustainable structure is greater than that of a conventional building, but that initial cost is recovered in the energy savings. The use of solar and wind for electricity production, the use of renewable materials such as wood for construction, and a significant reduction in the use of concrete (a major source of carbon) are all achievable. By LEED standards (Leadership in Energy and Environmental Design), simple registration and a Silver standard are easily realized, and a Gold standard produces a financial payback in about five years. The Platinum standard's (that is, zero carbon production's) payback is human survival itself.

We need governments to be more responsible and to demonstrate the political courage to be proactive. Cities could establish maximum energy consumption per square metre, as the Canadian federal government has done for its buildings. That initiative could be extended through city bylaws to apply to all buildings, as has been implemented in the Toronto Green Standard series of bylaws for new building applications. There is an urgent need for urban consolidation, especially for intensifying the density of suburban areas, rather than allowing cities to spread their footprint. An increase in density will render public transit viable and convenient, and reduce the amount of automobile traffic, a major source of greenhouse gas.

Two obstacles to sustainable design are the construction industry, which can be entrenched in its technologies, and the commercial interests of developers, which tend to be short-sighted. They both view sustainable design as an imposition.

Hope lies in the client. In the urban core, the dozens of condominiums that are under construction at any given moment tend to employ glass as the main external material. It is a relatively cheap way to build, and developers sell the view. But the four sides of the building aren't differentiated, so the southern and western exposures, where heat gain is acute, use the same materials as the shaded north and east sides. The cost of heating this inefficient design is passed on to the buyer. If buyers are given a choice, however, some will choose energy efficiency, paying more up front and reaping the future savings. In the absence of meaningful government action or even debate, and with the private sector not interested, the consumer is leading the way.

When DSAI designed the University of Ontario Institute of Technology (UOIT) in 2002 (Don Schmitt, principal in charge), we were lucky to have a client that embraced sustainable design. Our design included geothermal wells that are 183 metres deep. They provide cooling in summer and heat in the winter. They are augmented by a recovery system that recycles the heat generated by computers, lights, and people. The energy costs are much lower, and they are also stable — immune from the price fluctuations of oil and gas. The roofs are planted with vegetation to reduce solar heat gain, and to aid in the absorption of rainwater. The integrated design at UOIT extends to the treatment of storm water, which is usually collected in catch basins, piped to sewers, and on to treatment plants. Instead, at UOIT, heavy rains are collected in storm catchment ponds, where specific plants act as biofilters.

We also pioneered the use of biofilters to improve interior air quality. At the University of Guelph-Humber we applied a biofilter wall to the design — a living wall of tropical plants that includes orchids and bromeliads. It effectively deals with toxic interior air and reduces air conditioning costs. Greater investment in sustainable buildings will spur new technologies.

While the consumer can't lead the way when it comes to urban planning, citizens aren't powerless. In Toronto during the 1960s the looming argument between Toronto's core and the outlying suburbs turned into all-out war. Canada's first suburb was Toronto's Don Mills, built in the 1950s. The central idea was that it would be largely self-contained; at least half its residents would work there. This turned out to be optimistic, as only five percent of Don Mills residents worked there. As other suburbs have proliferated, the figure has dropped even lower; the vast majority of people living in the suburbs work in the urban core.

The Covid-19 pandemic, however, has opened up a very different option: with digital technology many can work effectively in remote locations. Once the pandemic is no longer determining our lives, it will be interesting to see whether working alone in remote locations continues to satisfy. What is crucially absent in such conditions is the informal interaction between members of firms or in other forms of employment. Often it is those interactions that produce the most effective results.

• • •

For suburban homeowners and politicians, the issue was how to get to the core quickly and easily. The answer was multi-lane highways. A highway was proposed to connect the main 401 Trans-Canada Highway with the downtown. The "Spadina Expressway" would result in the destruction of a thousand homes, the devaluation of thousands more, and the need for more central urban parking lots. It would fundamentally change the character of the city.

It became the central issue of the 1969 municipal election. Should a city be retrofitted to serve its suburbs? It was an epic battle for the future direction of the city — would Toronto, like many American cities, be hollowed at the core, spreading outward, or would it follow the European model, where the urban fabric is paramount. I, along with dozens of others, including urban theorist Jane Jacobs and future Toronto mayor John Sewell, argued vehemently against the expressway. There is evidence that the higher the volume of traffic through a neighbourhood, the lower the stability of the community. In 1971, we finally triumphed: the Spadina Expressway got no further than Eglinton Avenue, six kilometres north of downtown.

But the battle against unsustainable suburban sprawl goes on, both in Toronto and in cities across North America. This sprawl is unsustainable for several reasons. One is the enormous energy costs — both in the commutes (which can be four hours per day in the case of Toronto) and the energy inefficiencies of single-dwelling homes. Another is the cost of building and sustaining suburbs. Both hard services (utilities) and soft services (schools, libraries, clinics) cost more in suburban areas than in compact urban densities. For every dollar earned in property taxes in its low-density areas, Toronto pays $1.40 to service the land. Low density doesn't support public transit. If people need to drive to the subway station, they tend to take their car for the whole trip. Public transit has been woefully underfunded in most Canadian cities. The extra cost of operating a low-density city such as Toronto, compared to a compact city like Zurich or Vienna, is estimated at $1 billion annually.

. . .

The issue of sustainability is fundamentally one of concern for the public interest. Architects, along with other professionals, have their role to play. There is a moral obligation that distinguishes businesses and professionals. Professions have an ethical code of conduct and a moral responsibility, and individuals and companies do not. There are, of course, enlightened individuals and companies, but they have no obligation to serve the public interest. In the context of the built environment, their primary objective is to make money. Cities are built in the struggle between these competing values.

What a city builds, and gives prominence to, is a reflection of its culture and society. So when the Ontario government proposed building a casino on Toronto's waterfront, there was understandable opposition. The location was a prime public area. The argument in favour of the casino was that it would be a tourist attraction and an economic boon. This was a false argument; studies have shown that there is a net economic loss in neighbourhoods with casinos. Apart from the amorality of casinos — the house always wins, and instead of taxing those who can afford it, casinos tend to victimize the lower-income component of society — they are also hermetically sealed environments that discourage any other development, including restaurants and shops. They take pedestrian traffic off the streets. A well-thought-out waterfront development would provide social and economic benefits. A casino would provide neither.

There were, as might be expected, powerful individuals in support of the casino. In opposition, a committee was formed around a blunt slogan: No Casino. Members included city councillors, representatives of social interest organizations, and

well-intentioned individuals. Diamond Schmitt's main conference room became the campaign headquarters.

We developed a strategy that was both positive and negative. The negative one was to plaster *No Casino* signs in the
wards of city councillors who were in support of the casino.
We met with the editorial boards of the principal newspapers,
had respected community leaders speak out, and held a press
conference at city hall with fifty religious leaders, including the
archbishop of the Catholic Church in Toronto. In the end, the
project was rejected.

. . .

Another ill-advised planning initiative was a proposed airport
in the town of Pickering, east of Toronto. The idea was that it
would relieve some of the air traffic from Pearson, the city's
main airport. Pickering is a highly productive agricultural area,
but by 1973 the federal government had already expropriated
all the farmland necessary for the airport. Preliminary construction began, but stopped in 1975. A revised airport proposal was the subject of an Ontario Municipal Board hearing, and
I appeared as an "expert witness." I emphasized that if the intention was to relieve the Toronto airport of short-haul traffic,
a high-speed rail service would be more effective, have wider
economic benefits, and, importantly, would conserve valuable
agricultural land. It was also counterintuitive to service short-
haul routes to and from an airport that is an hour from the
city's core: travellers don't want to spend more time on the
commute to and from the airport than in the air.

The glacial speed of bureaucracies is a double-edged
sword. The plans for the airport were developed in the late

1960s and gained some traction in the 1970s, though they proceeded slowly during that period. Between then and now, Toronto's main airport has undergone a massive expansion that will service the needs of the city for several decades. The strenuous opposition to the Pickering project was based on logic. An airport there would disrupt the community, destroy farmland, and only yield a two-runway airport. It would also further clog the already congested 401 Highway (one of the busiest in North America) with unnecessary traffic. At any rate, the reasons for building the airport had been chiefly political. In 1972, Transport Minister Jean Marchand said that he didn't want to be the "French Canadian who could be accused of not giving an airport to Ontario after having given one to Quebec" (the ill-fated Mirabel). In the end, the Pickering project was cancelled. However, the Federal Government has retained ownership of the lands. Citizens must be ever watchful.

. . .

We also need governments to take a long-term view and look beyond partisan lines. In 1995, the premier of Ontario, Bob Rae, realized that the growth of metropolitan Toronto required a comprehensive assessment of policies governing land use, transportation, governance, and taxation of the greater Toronto area. A commission was set up to undertake this work. Five commissioners were appointed, $3 million assigned to cover the costs of research and consulting fees for expert advice and staff to administrate the enterprise. Anne Golden was appointed the chairperson, with Rob Prichard, president of the University of Toronto, Dr. Joseph Wong, a prominent member of the Chinese community, Tom McCormack, an economist, and myself as commissioners.

Our first discovery was that the census statistics did not distinguish between urban and rural settlement. The first task was therefore to recast the figures on a geographical basis. The growth of Toronto had been accompanied by enlightened governance systems, and an appropriately scaled infrastructure. Our aim was to take it to the next step, commensurate with its size and economy. In effect, to achieve regional integration and integration with the global economy. Our conclusions amounted to fifty-one recommendations. Those, if implemented, would establish Toronto globally as one of the best urban areas in which to live, work, and play.

However, shortly after what became known as the Golden Report, the New Democratic Party was defeated by the Conservative party with Mike Harris as premier. The electorate in support of the Conservatives was more suburban, small town, and rural. Our report was shelved. We are still suffering the consequences of that decision made on right-wing ideological grounds, and not on the merits of the report.

. . .

A new challenge has arrived in the form of pandemics. We've seen the damage done globally by the coronavirus in just a few weeks and how cities were hit particularly hard. Cities are where pandemics tend to start, but they are also where the expertise, facilities, and budgets exist to fight them. And cities may be the first areas to emerge with some degree of immunity, as London did during the smallpox plague of the eighteenth century.

As is so often the case in planning and design, there is a need to resolve new opposing demands: how to make cities dense, but safe. Following the pandemic, there will be fundamental anthropological change. A sufficient change in degree entails a change in kind: the massive migration of populations to prime urban centres will need an urgent new calibration.

. . .

There is much that architecture and urban planning can do to improve the lives of citizens, mitigate climate change and decrease environmental degradation. The enemies are ignorance, bureaucracy, greed, and complacency — familiar foes. But today, the consequences of inaction are dire.

Architects have an ethical and moral obligation to take the public interest into account. We also have the exceptional professional ability to act at the micro, mezzo, and macro scales. In the current era, climate change constitutes an existential threat; huge disparity in incomes has meant the inadequacy of housing for the poor; and dispersal of immigrants to the perimeter of cities, with inadequate social services, has sidelined them. As architects, we are blessed with the ability to address these and other pressing issues. Their resolution would be as great as any design achievement. Indeed, how privileged we are to have such potential. Realizing such potential will inevitably provide profound personal and public satisfaction. It is within our power to obey the Old Testament dictum *tikkun olam*, "to make a better world."

Acknowledgements

IN THE PREPARATION OF MY MEMOIR THE CONTRIBUTION of others has been of the greatest value. Many thanks go to Don Gillmor for his editing, which not only greatly improved the text, but its sequence; Tania Freeman, for her salient contribution, providing structure and clarity; Elizabeth Gyde, art director of Diamond Schmitt, for her improvement to, and production of, the images; Sona Samlal, my unflappable assistant, who retrieved long past articles I wrote and typed and retyped the manuscript; Michael Leckman, for the production and intelligibility of the family tree; Michael Levine, for his advice and patience regarding publication; Jeanette Parker, for her clarity and discipline regarding publication edits; and to Marta Braun and Juli Morrow, who both reviewed and provided constructive advice on early versions of the text.

I owe the greatest debt of all to the forbearance and encouragement of my wife, Gillian. Without her love, devotion, and tolerance, none of my achievements would have been possible.

About the Author

ABEL JOSEPH (JACK) DIAMOND WAS BORN IN HIS GRAND-
father's study in the town of Piet Retief, South Africa. He
received a Bachelor of Architecture, with Distinction, from
the University of Cape Town; a Master of Arts from Oxford
University; a Master of Architecture from the University of
Pennsylvania; and honourary doctorates from DalTech,
Dalhousie University, and the University of Toronto. He is a
fellow of the Royal Architectural Institute of Canada and the
Canadian Institute of Planners, an RAIC Gold Medallist, an
honourary fellow of the American Institute of Architects, an
Officer of the Order of Canada, and a member of the Order of
Ontario. Jack received the Jane Jacobs Lifetime Achievement
Award and the Ontario Association of Architects Award, and
his firm was placed in the top ten globally in the cultural sec-
tor by *World Architecture*. He was a member of the University
of Cape Town rugby team, the combined university teams of
Cape Town and Stellenbosch on their European tour, and an
Oxford rugby Blue. While unable to participate, he was select-
ed for the Springbok rugby trials for the 1957 tour of Australia.